Lickety-Split QUILTS for Little Ones

Martingale®
& COMPANY

Lickety-Split Quilts
for Little Ones

Laurie Bevan

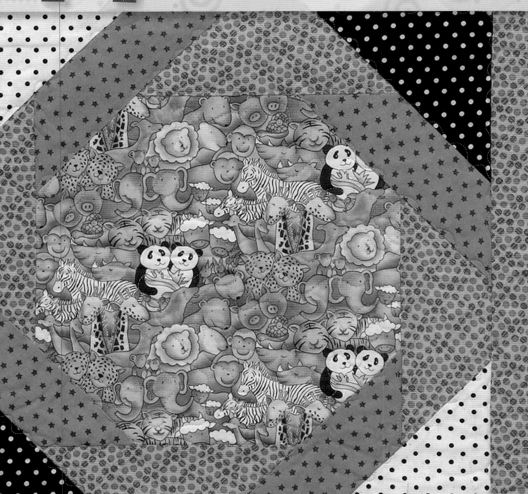

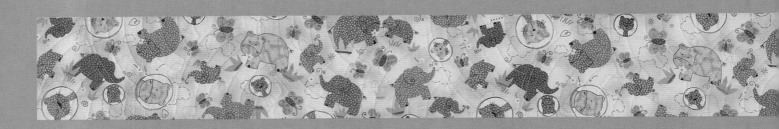

Lickety-Split Quilts for Little Ones
© 2007 by Laurie Bevan

That Patchwork Place® is an imprint of
Martingale & Company®.

Martingale & Company
20205 144th Ave. NE
Woodinville, WA 98072-8478 USA
www.martingale-pub.com

Credits

President & CEO ....Tom Wierzbicki
Publisher ....Jane Hamada
Editorial Director ....Mary V. Green
Managing Editor ....Tina Cook
Developmental Editor...............Karen Costello Soltys
Technical Editor...........................Ellen Pahl
Copy Editor ....Liz McGehee
Design Director............................Stan Green
Assistant Design Director ....Regina Girard
Illustrator ....Robin Strobel
Cover & Text Designer ....Stan Green
Photographer...............................Brent Kane

Printed in China
12 11 10 09 08 07   8 7 6 5 4 3 2 1

Library of Congress Cataloging-in-Publication Data
Library of Congress Control Number: 2007009511

ISBN: 978-1-56477-721-8

Mission Statement
Dedicated to providing quality products and service
to inspire creativity.

Dedication

To my parents, thanks for everything, and I do mean everything!

Acknowledgments

Thanks to the wonderful women who pieced some of these quilts: Suzanne Kolhagen, Suzanne Nelson, Laura Roberts, and Tess Robinson. I appreciate your support, and I could never have finished them all on time without you.

I am a quiltmaker, but my husband calls me a "topper," so thanks to the talented quilters who take care of the quilting for me: Shirley Bowen, Karen Ford, Ann Jones, Dawn Kelly, and Virginia Lauth. Your beautiful stitches turn my tops into quilts.

I couldn't design all these quilts without soliciting lots of advice and opinions, so thanks to the Slumber Party Girls—you know who you are.

Thank you to my editors, Ellen and Liz. I write it, and you make sure it's right.

Martingale & Company is staffed by creative women and men who publish beautiful quilt books. I am so proud to be one of your authors.

I would like to thank the following companies for providing me with lots of lovely fabrics to use in my quilts: Andover Fabrics; The Erlanger Group, Ltd.; Fabric Country/Classic Cottons; Northcott Silk, Inc.; and Robert Kaufman Fabrics.

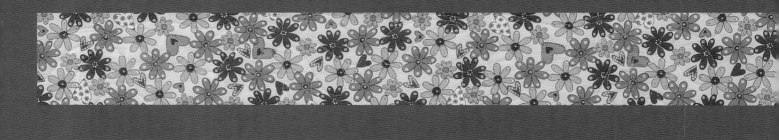

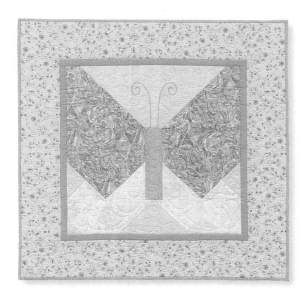

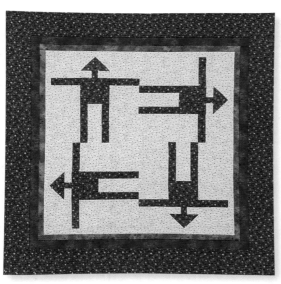

Contents

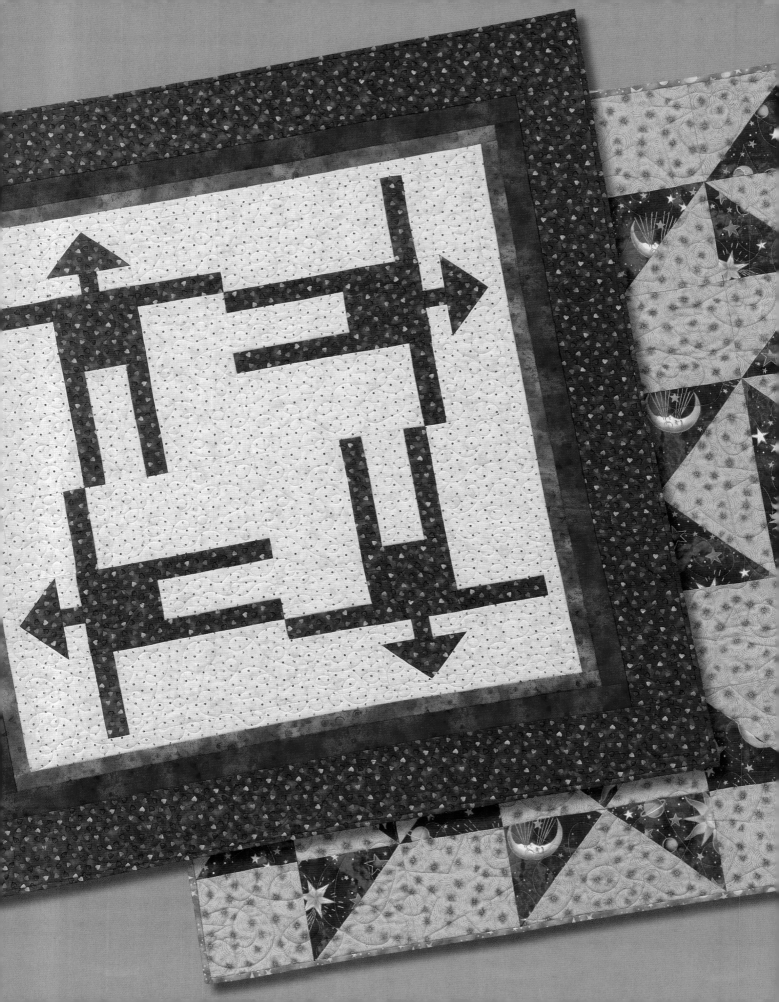

Introduction

Lickety-split means "with great speed." Is there anything in our lives today that doesn't need to be done with great speed?

I have to laugh when I hear stories from quilters who are making baby quilts. They have known for months that the baby is coming, yet sometimes the baby is celebrating the first birthday before he or she receives the quilt. Here's your chance to make those baby quilts lickety-split!

Fifteen different blocks are presented. I have chosen blocks that are unusual and more interesting than blocks normally used to make baby quilts. Since the blocks are larger than what might be considered standard for a baby quilt, that means there are fewer blocks in each quilt, so it is important to choose a more interesting-looking block. Instead of the Nine Patch block, I have used the Rolling Nine Patch block to make "Rolling Blocks" on page 28. Take a look at "Waddlin' Around" on page 50. The center of this quilt is made using the Grandma's Hopscotch block. The resources I used in my search for blocks are listed in the bibliography on page 77.

Many times, the first quilt a beginning quilter makes is a baby quilt; and if we in the industry of quiltmaking are lucky, it will be the first of many quilts. Most, if not all, of the quilts in this book are simple enough for a beginner. Anyone with just a little experience will be able to make any of them.

These quilts were designed to be used and loved. What greater satisfaction can you have than knowing the quilt you made is going everywhere with the baby? I hope you enjoy making lickety-split quilts to be loved by the special little ones in your life.

The "Rolling Blocks" quilt used four Rolling Nine Patch blocks. See page 28 for project instructions.

The Big-Block Baby Quilt

It doesn't take many big blocks to make a baby quilt. Several of the quilts in this book are made using only one big block, and many of the quilts are made using just four blocks. Imagine how fast your baby quilt will be finished if you only have to make one or even four blocks!

Designing Your Own Big Blocks

Many standard blocks can be enlarged to become big blocks. Choose simple blocks without too many pieces and ones that are made up of units that can be sewn with easy piecing techniques. Squirrel in a Cage, Baby Bunting, and Rolling Nine Patch are good choices for big blocks. More complex blocks work well in a single big-block quilt, as you can see with the Double Dutch block that was used to make the "Double Dutch" quilt on page 47. I made the finished block 24" x 24", so the many smaller pieces are still very simple to sew, and you only have to make one block for a baby quilt that's the perfect size.

Take some time to browse through the books listed in the bibliography on page 77 to find wonderful blocks to use in your own baby-quilt designs. To enlarge a block, follow these easy steps.

1. Choose a block and determine on which grid your block is built: three, four, or five. The number of grid units should be the same across and down, and each grid unit should be the same size. The grid unit is highlighted in each of these sample blocks (above right). For example, if the Squirrel in a Cage block is based on a 3 x 3 grid and it is 9" finished, then each grid unit is 3" x 3" finished.

2. Once you know the grid your block is based on, you can enlarge it to any size you want. Decide how big you want each finished grid unit to be and multiply that by the grid number to equal the finished size of your block. Using the previous blocks as examples, you can see how this works.

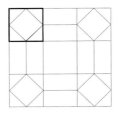

Squirrel in a Cage,
a 3-unit grid

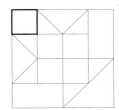

Baby Bunting,
a 4-unit grid

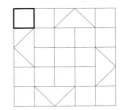

Rolling Nine Patch,
a 5-unit grid

Squirrel in a Cage: Each grid unit will finish to 5"; it is a three-grid block.
5 x 3 = 15" finished block

Baby Bunting: Each grid unit will finish to 4"; it is a four-grid block.
4 x 4 = 16" finished block

Rolling Nine Patch: Each grid unit will finish to 3"; it is a five-grid block.
3 x 5 = 15" finished block

3. Cut and sew the grid units so they will finish to the size you have chosen.

You can have a lot of fun creating big blocks. Please don't let the math intimidate you; it's really quite easy.

Bugs in the Barn

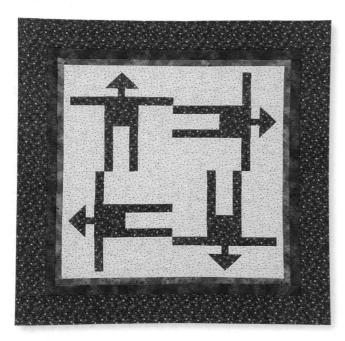

The Tin Man

Big Baby Quilts

Once your big blocks are made, it's time to sew them into a baby quilt. Now you have a decision to make. How big do you want your quilt to be? The quilt you're designing is for a baby, so don't get carried away and make it too big. The perfect size is from 40" up to 48", and the quilt shape can be either a square or a rectangle.

Try one of the following techniques to make your quilt the perfect size. Add simple sashing strips as in "Bugs in the Barn" shown at left. Add sashing strips and cornerstones as in "Ducky Playtime" on page 13. Add three different-sized borders as in "Animal Friends" on page 60 and "The Tin Man" shown at left. Turn your blocks on point as in "Sweet Rosebuds" on page 32. Add a large outer border of the cute print you've chosen for your quilt as in "Waddlin' Around" on page 50. Be careful not to overdo it though. A border that is too large in proportion to the center of the quilt will not enhance your quilt design; it will just look as if you were trying to make your quilt bigger. Choose any one of these techniques, or a combination of them, to complement your blocks and make a quilt the baby will love.

I hope you will feel inspired to design your own lickety-split baby quilt very soon. We have such wonderful fabric choices for baby quilts, why stop at just one? You never know when that next baby is due!

Ducky Playtime

 By Laurie Bevan. Quilted by Karen Ford, Poulsbo, Washington.
- **Quilt Size: 45" x 45"**
- **Block Size: 15" x 15"**
- **Block Name: Squirrel in a Cage**

Have fun choosing a charming 1930s reproduction print and combine it with old-fashioned muslin to make a very traditional and appealing baby quilt. The lucky baby who receives this quilt will enjoy naptime as much as playtime.

Materials

Yardage is based on 42"-wide fabric.

- ◆ 1⅛ yards of large-scale duck print for blocks and outer border
- ◆ ⅔ yard of dotted duck print for blocks and binding
- ◆ ⅔ yard of yellow print for blocks
- ◆ ½ yard of muslin for sashing
- ◆ ⅛ yard of red print for cornerstones
- ◆ 2¾ yards of fabric for backing
- ◆ 49" x 49" piece of batting

Cutting

All measurements include ¼"-wide seam allowances. Instructions are for cutting strips across the fabric width.

From the yellow print, cut:
3 strips, 3⅜" x 42"; crosscut into 32 squares, 3⅜" x 3⅜". Cut each square once diagonally to yield 64 triangles.

3 strips, 3" x 42"

From the large-scale duck print, cut:
5 strips, 5½" x 42"; crosscut *1 strip* into 4 squares, 5½" x 5½". (Save remainder of strips for outer border.)

2 strips, 4" x 42"; crosscut into 16 squares, 4" x 4"

From the dotted duck print, cut:
3 strips, 3" x 42"

5 strips, 2¼" x 42"

From the muslin, cut:
6 strips, 2" x 42"; crosscut into 12 pieces, 2" x 15½"

From the red print, cut:
1 strip, 2" x 42"; crosscut into 9 squares, 2" x 2"

Making the Blocks

After each sewing step, press the seam allowances as directed by the arrows in the illustration.

1. Sew the yellow triangles to the sides of each 4" duck-print square to make the corner units.

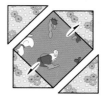

Make 16.

2. Sew together the 3"-wide yellow and dotted strips along the strip length. Make a total of three strip sets. Crosscut the strip sets into 16 segments, 5½" wide. These are the side units.

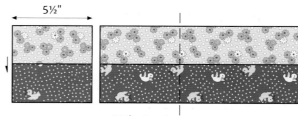

Make 3 strip sets.
Cut 16 segments.

3. Arrange and sew together one 5½" duck-print square, four of the corner units from step 1, and four of the side units from step 2 as shown to make one block. Make a total of four blocks.

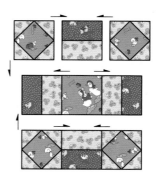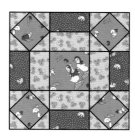

Make 4.

Assembling the Quilt Top

1. Arrange and sew together the four blocks, the 15½"-long muslin strips, and the red squares as shown.

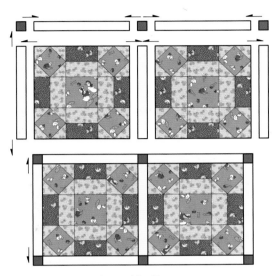

Assembly diagram

2. Referring to "Adding Borders" on page 71, attach the 5½"-wide duck-print outer-border strips to the quilt top. Border lengths should be:
   Side border strips: 35" each
   Top and bottom border strips: 45" each

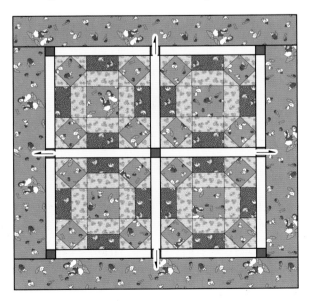

Finishing

Refer to the quilt finishing techniques on pages 72–76 for detailed instructions if needed.

1. Piece the quilt backing (if necessary) so that it is approximately 4" wider and longer than the quilt top. Mark the quilt top if desired.

2. Layer the quilt top with batting and backing, and baste the layers together. Hand or machine quilt as desired.

3. Trim the batting and backing even with the edges of the quilt top. Add a hanging sleeve if desired. Using the 2¼"-wide dotted strips, prepare the binding and sew it to the quilt. Make a label and attach it to your quilt.

Wish on a Star

By Laurie Bevan. Quilted by Ann Jones, Poulsbo, Washington.
- **Quilt Size: 40½" x 40½"**
- **Block Size: 20" x 20"**
- **Block Name: Crystal Star**

Your darling baby will sleep like an angel under this celestial quilt. It is made of one big block with half-block and quarter-block sections around it. If you don't see the block sections, take a look at the assembly diagram on page 19, and you'll see what I mean. All you have to do is choose one heavenly print and a coordinating background fabric; then cut and sew. Sweet dreams!

Materials

Yardage is based on 42"-wide fabric.

+ 1½ yards of turquoise print for background
+ 1¼ yards of celestial print for blocks
+ ⅜ yard of gold print for binding
+ 2½ yards of fabric for backing
+ 45" x 45" piece of batting

Cutting

All measurements include ¼"-wide seam allowances. Instructions are for cutting strips across the fabric width.

From the turquoise print, cut:
2 strips, 5⅞" x 42"; crosscut into 12 squares, 5⅞" x 5⅞". Cut *2 squares* once diagonally to yield 4 triangles.
6 strips, 5½" x 42"; crosscut into:
    8 rectangles, 5½" x 10½"
    24 squares, 5½" x 5½"

From the celestial print, cut:
1 strip, 10½" x 42"; crosscut into:
    4 rectangles, 5½" x 10½"

    From the remainder of the strip, cut 1 square, 7⅝" x 7⅝"

2 strips, 5⅞" x 42"; crosscut into 10 squares, 5⅞" x 5⅞"

3 strips, 5½" x 42"; crosscut into 16 squares, 5½" x 5½"

From the gold print, cut:
5 strips, 2¼" x 42"

Making the Quilt Top

After each sewing step, press the seam allowances as directed by the arrows in the illustration.

1. Sew a turquoise triangle to each side of the 7⅝" celestial square.

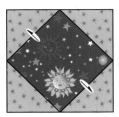

Make 1.

2. Draw a diagonal line on the wrong side of each 5½" celestial square. With right sides together, place a square at one end of each turquoise rectangle. Sew on the diagonal line. Trim ¼" from the stitched line and press the seam. Place another square at the opposite end of each rectangle. Be sure the diagonal line is oriented in the opposite direction of the first square. Sew, trim, and press as before.

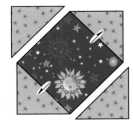

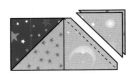
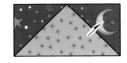

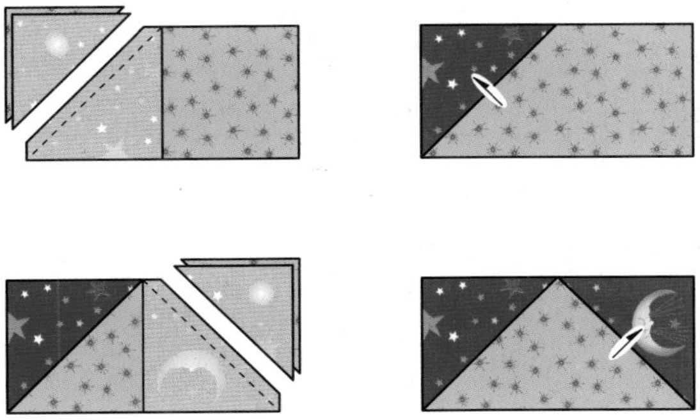

Make 8.

3. Repeat step 2, using eight of the 5½" turquoise squares and the celestial rectangles.

Make 4.

4. Draw a diagonal line on the wrong side of the 5⅞" turquoise squares. Place the squares right sides together with the 5⅞" celestial squares. Sew ¼" from each side of the drawn line. Cut the squares apart on the line and press.

Make 20.

5. Sew a 5½" turquoise square to each side of six of the units from step 2.

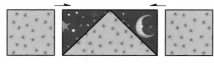

Make 6.

6. Arrange and sew together the unit from step 1, the two remaining units from step 2, and two units from step 5 as shown to make the center block.

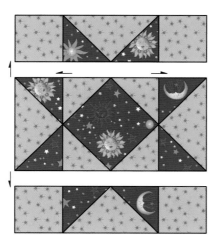

Make 1.

7. Sew a unit from step 4 to each side of the four units from step 3 as shown.

Make 4.

8. Sew the four units from steps 5 and 7 together in pairs as shown.

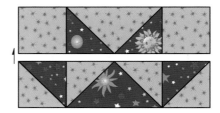

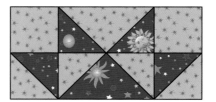

Make 4.

9. Sew three units from step 4 and one 5½" turquoise square together as shown.

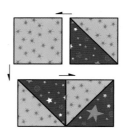 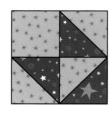

Make 4.

10. Arrange and sew together the block from step 6 and the block sections from steps 8 and 9 as shown.

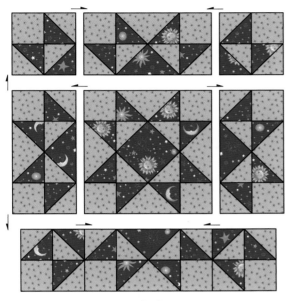

Assembly diagram

Finishing

Refer to the quilt finishing techniques on pages 72–76 for detailed instructions if needed.

1. Piece the quilt backing (if necessary) so that it is approximately 4" wider and longer than the quilt top. Mark the quilt top if necessary.

2. Layer the quilt top with batting and backing, and baste the layers together. Hand or machine quilt as desired.

3. Trim the batting and backing even with the edges of the quilt top. Add a hanging sleeve if desired. Using the 2¼"-wide gold strips, prepare the binding and sew it to the quilt. Make a label and attach it to your quilt.

GROWN-UP QUILT IDEA

This design will also make a beautiful wall hanging or small table topper. Try using a gorgeous floral fabric with a subtle, coordinating background print. Or how about a traditional two-color quilt of red and white or blue and white? For a great gift idea, just use two fabrics that match the recipient's home decor.

Bugs in the Barn

Designed by Laurie Bevan. Pieced by Suzanne Nelson, Kenmore, Washington.
Quilted by Karen Ford, Poulsbo, Washington.

- **Quilt Size:** 45½" x 45½"
- **Block Size:** 16" x 16"
- **Block Name:** Hole in the Barn Door

I fell in love with this bug fabric and knew that I wanted to use it in this quilt. The bright colors together with the happy bug print make such a cheerful quilt. Thanks go to Suzanne for making this quilt—it's perfect for either a baby girl or a baby boy.

Materials

Yardage is based on 42"-wide fabric.

+ 1⅛ yards of bug print for blocks and outer border
+ ⅔ yard of red dot for sashing and inner border
+ ½ yard of yellow dot for blocks
+ ⅜ yard of blue dot for blocks
+ ⅜ yard of green dot for blocks
+ ½ yard of red-with-black dot for binding
+ 2⅞ yards of backing fabric
+ 50" x 50" piece of batting

Cutting

All measurements include ¼"-wide seam allowances. Instructions are for cutting strips across the fabric width.

From the yellow dot, cut:
1 strip, 4⅞" x 42"; crosscut into 8 squares, 4⅞" x 4⅞"

4 strips, 2½" x 42"

From the blue dot, cut:
1 strip, 4⅞" x 42"; crosscut into 4 squares, 4⅞" x 4⅞"

2 strips, 2½" x 42"

From the green dot, cut:
1 strip, 4⅞" x 42"; crosscut into 4 squares, 4⅞" x 4⅞"

2 strips, 2½" x 42"

From the bug print, cut:
1 strip, 8½" x 42"; crosscut into 4 squares, 8½" x 8½"

4 strips, 4½" x 42"

2 squares, 6⅞" x 6⅞"

From the red dot, cut:
2 strips, 1½" x 42"; crosscut into:
    2 strips, 1½" x 16½"
    1 strip, 1½" x 33½"

4 strips, 2½" x 42"

2 squares, 6⅞" x 6⅞"

From the red-with-black dot, cut:
5 strips, 2¼" x 42"

Making the Blocks

After each sewing step, press the seam allowances as directed by the arrows in the illustration.

1. Draw a diagonal line on the wrong side of each 4⅞" yellow square. Place the squares right sides together with each 4⅞" blue and green square. Sew ¼" from each side of the drawn line. Cut the squares apart on the line and press.

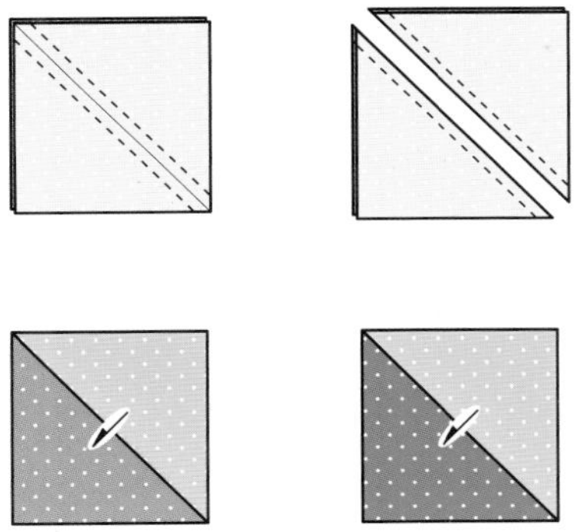

Make 8.   Make 8.

2. Sew a 2½"-wide yellow strip to a blue strip lengthwise as shown. Make two strip sets and cut them into eight segments, 8½" long.

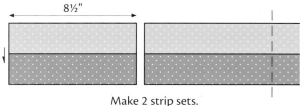

Make 2 strip sets.
Cut 8 segments.

3. Sew a 2½"-wide yellow strip to a green strip lengthwise as shown. Make two strip sets and cut them into eight segments, 8½" long.

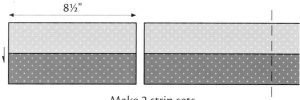

Make 2 strip sets.
Cut 8 segments.

4. Sew the units and 8½" bug squares together as shown to make two blue blocks and two green blocks.

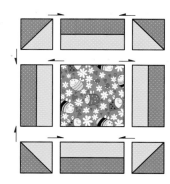

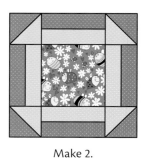

Make 2.   Make 2.

Assembling the Quilt Top

1. Sew the four blocks and the 1½"-wide red strips together as shown.

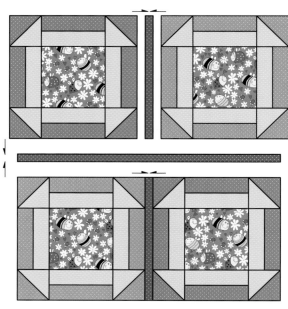

Assembly diagram

2. Draw a diagonal line on the wrong side of each 6⅞" red square. Place each square right sides together with a 6⅞" bug square. Sew ¼" from each side of the drawn line. Cut the squares apart on the line and press.

Make 4.

3. Sew a 2½"-wide red strip to a 4½"-wide bug strip lengthwise as shown. Make four strip sets and cut each to a length of 33½".

Make 4 strip sets.
Trim each to 33½" long.

4. Sew two of the strips from step 3 to the sides of the quilt center. Sew the triangle squares from step 2 to the ends of the two remaining strips from step 3 as shown. Sew these strips to the top and bottom of the quilt.

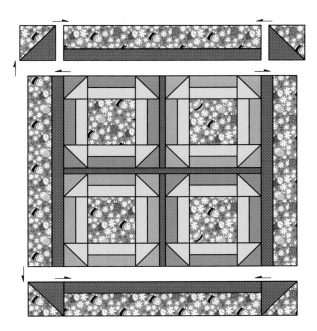

Finishing

Refer to the quilt finishing techniques on pages 72–76 for detailed instructions if needed.

1. Piece the quilt backing (if necessary) so that it is approximately 4" wider and longer than the quilt top. Mark the quilt top if necessary.

2. Layer the quilt top with batting and backing, and baste the layers together. Hand or machine quilt as desired.

3. Trim the batting and backing even with the edges of the quilt top. Add a hanging sleeve if desired. Using the 2¼"-wide red-with-black strips, prepare the binding and sew it to the quilt. Make a label and attach it to your quilt.

PHOTO QUILT IDEA

Find four terrific family photos, print them on fabric, and use them in place of the 8½" bug print squares. Choose fabrics for the other pieces that will reflect the mood you're trying to create with your quilt.

Beautiful Butterfly

 By Laurie Bevan. Quilted by Dawn Kelly, Ponderay, Idaho.
- **Quilt Size: 30½" x 30½"**
- **Block Size: 20" x 20"**
- **Block Name: Butterfly**

Make this beautiful quilt as a wall hanging for the baby's nursery or use it as the perfect little cradle quilt. When your baby girl gets a little older, she can comfort her dolls and wrap them up with this pretty quilt.

Materials

Yardage is based on 42"-wide fabric.

+ ⅝ yard of yellow butterfly print for outer border
+ ½ yard of pink print for body and binding
+ ⅜ yard of multicolored swirl print for upper wing
+ ⅓ yard of yellow print for background
+ ¼ yard of pink frosted fabric for lower wing
+ ¼ yard of green dot for inner border
+ 1 yard of fabric for backing
+ 35" x 35" piece of batting
+ Pink embroidery floss or permanent marker for antennae

Cutting

All measurements include ¼"-wide seam allowances. Instructions are for cutting strips across the fabric width.

From the multicolored swirl print, cut:
2 rectangles, 9" x 9½"
2 rectangles, 8" x 9½"

From the yellow print, cut:
1 rectangle, 8" x 17½"
1 rectangle, 4½" x 8½"
1 square, 5⅜" x 5⅜"

From the pink frosted fabric, cut:
1 square, 5⅜" x 5⅜"
2 squares, 5" x 5"
2 rectangles, 4½" x 10½"

From the pink print, cut:
1 piece, 2½" x 9"
4 strips, 2¼" x 42"

From the green dot, cut:
4 strips, 1½" x 42"

From the yellow butterfly print, cut:
4 strips, 4½" x 42"

Making the Block

After each sewing step, press the seam allowances as directed by the arrows in the illustration.

1. Place an 8" x 9½" swirl-print rectangle right sides together with the 8" x 17½" yellow rectangle, matching two raw edges as shown. Draw a diagonal line from the corner of the background piece to the corner of the wing piece. This is a 45° angle. Sew on the drawn line, starting at the corner of the swirl-print wing piece. Trim ¼" from the stitched line and press.

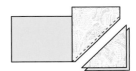

2. Repeat step 1, using the other 8" x 9½" swirl-print rectangle placed at the other end of the yellow rectangle as shown. Sew, trim, and press as before to make section A.

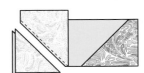

Section A

3. Draw a diagonal line on the wrong side of the 5⅜" yellow square. Place the square right sides together with the 5⅜" pink-frosted square. Sew ¼" from each side of the drawn line. Cut the squares apart on the line and press. Draw a diagonal line perpendicular to the seam line on the wrong side of each triangle square.

Make 2.

4. Place one triangle square from step 3 on one corner of a 9" x 9½" swirl-print rectangle as shown. This rectangle looks like a square, so be sure the triangle square is in the correct corner. Sew on the drawn line. Trim ¼" from the stitched line and press.

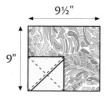

9½"

9"

5. Draw a diagonal line on the wrong side of each 5" pink-frosted square. With right sides together, place a marked square at the adjacent corner on the piece from step 4. Once again, be sure the square is in the correct corner. Sew, trim, and press as before to make the left side of section B.

Left section B

6. Repeat steps 4 and 5, using the remaining 9" x 9½" swirl-print rectangle, the other triangle square from step 3, and the last 5" pink-frosted square to make the right side of section B. Note that the pieces are added on the opposite sides.

9½"

9"

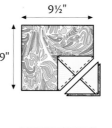

Right section B

7. Sew the left and right sides of section B to opposite sides of the 2½" x 9" pink print piece as shown to complete section B.

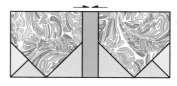

Section B

8. Place a 4½" x 10½" pink-frosted rectangle right sides together with the 4½" x 8½" yellow rectangle, matching two raw edges as shown. Draw a diagonal line from the corner of the background piece to the corner of the wing piece as in step 1. This is a 45° angle. Sew on the

drawn line, starting at the corner of the wing piece. Trim ¼" from the stitched line and press.

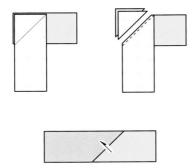

9. Place the second 4½" x 10½" pink-frosted rectangle at the other end of the unit from step 8 as shown. Sew, trim, and press as before to make section C.

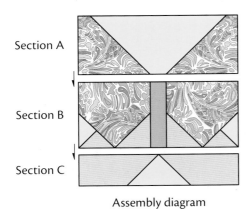

Section C

10. Arrange and sew together sections A, B, and C as shown.

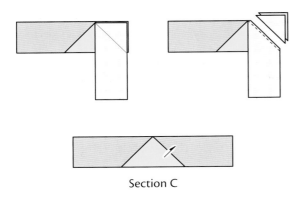

Section A

Section B

Section C

Assembly diagram

11. Using the antenna pattern on page 76, trace two antennae onto the Butterfly block, using the photo on page 24 as a guide for placement. Use an outline stitch and three strands of pink embroidery floss to stitch the antennae. If you

prefer, you may stitch the antennae by machine, using a narrow zigzag stitch, or simply draw the antennae, using a permanent marker.

Assembling the Quilt Top

Referring to "Adding Borders" on page 71, attach the 1½"-wide green inner-border strips and the 4½"-wide yellow butterfly outer-border strips to the quilt top. Border lengths should be:
   Inner-border strips: 20½" each for sides; 22½" each for top and bottom
   Outer-border strips: 22½" each for sides; 30½" each for top and bottom

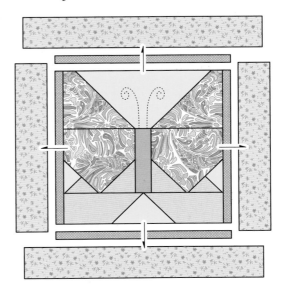

Finishing

Refer to the quilt finishing techniques on pages 72–76 for detailed instructions if needed.

1. Cut the quilt backing so that it is approximately 4" wider and longer than the quilt top. Mark the quilt top if necessary.

2. Layer the quilt top with batting and backing, and baste the layers together. Hand or machine quilt as desired.

3. Trim the batting and backing even with the edges of the quilt top. Add a hanging sleeve if desired. Using the 2¼"-wide pink strips, prepare the binding and sew it to the quilt. Make a label and attach it to your quilt.

Rolling Blocks

Designed by Laurie Bevan. Pieced by Tess Robinson, St. Joseph, Michigan. Quilted by Dawn Kelly, Ponderay, Idaho.

- **Quilt Size: 40½" x 40½"**
- **Block Size: 15" x 15"**
- **Block Name: Rolling Nine Patch**

All the fabrics in this quilt are from one collection, which means they were all made to coordinate. This is a very easy way of choosing fabrics for a quilt because these collections are usually displayed together at quilt shops. Thank you, Tess, for doing a great job of showcasing this collection.

Materials

Yardage is based on 42"-wide fabric.

+ 1 yard of green floral for outer border and binding
+ ⅔ yard of white swirl print for blocks
+ ⅜ yard of pink circle print for blocks
+ ¼ yard of green circle print for blocks
+ ¼ yard of purple circle print for blocks
+ ¼ yard of purple stripe for inner border
+ ¼ yard of green print for blocks
+ ¼ yard of purple print for blocks
+ 2½ yards of backing fabric
+ 45" x 45" piece of batting

Cutting

All measurements include ¼"-wide seam allowances. Instructions are for cutting strips across the fabric width.

From the white swirl print, cut:
6 strips, 3½" x 42"; crosscut into 64 squares, 3½" x 3½"

From the pink circle print, cut:
1 strip, 3½" x 42"; crosscut into 10 squares, 3½" x 3½"

1 strip, 6½" x 42"; crosscut into 8 rectangles, 3½" x 6½"

From the purple print, cut:
1 strip, 3½" x 42"; crosscut into 8 squares, 3½" x 3½"

From the green circle print, cut:
2 strips, 3½" x 42"; crosscut into:
    5 squares, 3½" x 3½"
    4 rectangles, 3½" x 6½"

From the purple circle print, cut:
2 strips, 3½" x 42"; crosscut into:
    5 squares, 3½" x 3½"
    4 rectangles, 3½" x 6½"

From the green print, cut:
1 strip, 3½" x 42"; crosscut into 8 squares, 3½" x 3½"

From the purple stripe, cut:
4 strips, 1½" x 42"

From the green floral, cut:
4 strips, 4½" x 42"

5 strips, 2¼" x 42"

Making the Blocks

After each sewing step, press the seam allowances as directed by the arrows in the illustration.

1. Make two nine-patch units, using 8 white squares and 10 pink squares as shown.

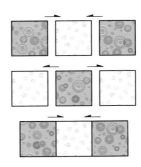 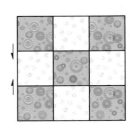

Make 2.

2. Draw a diagonal line on the wrong side of 16 white squares. With right sides together, place a white square at one end of each pink rectangle. Sew on the diagonal line. Trim ¼" from the stitched line and press. Place another white square at the opposite end of each rectangle. Be sure the diagonal line is oriented in the opposite direction of the first square. Sew, trim, and press as before to make eight flying-geese units.

Make 8.

3. Sew a white square to one side of each pink flying-geese unit as shown.

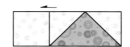

Make 8.

4. Sew a unit from step 3 to each side of the nine-patch units from step 1 as shown. Sew a purple print square to each end of the remaining units from step 3 and sew these units to the top and bottom of each block.

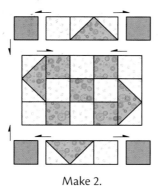

Make 2.

5. Repeat steps 1–4, using white squares and the green circle and purple circle squares and rectangles to make one green and one purple block. Use green print squares in place of the

purple squares in step 4 to make the block corners and press the seams in step 4 in the opposite direction from the pink blocks.

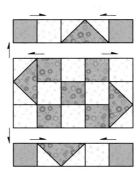

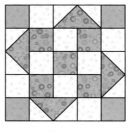
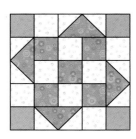

Make 1.   Make 1.

Assembling the Quilt Top

1. Sew the four blocks together as shown.

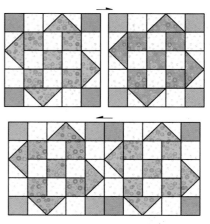

Assembly diagram

2. Referring to "Adding Borders" on page 71, attach the 1½"-wide purple inner-border strips and the 4½"-wide green outer-border strips to the quilt top. Border lengths should be as shown below.

Inner-border strips: 30½" each for sides; 32½" each for top and bottom

Outer-border strips: 32½" each for sides; 40½" each for top and bottom

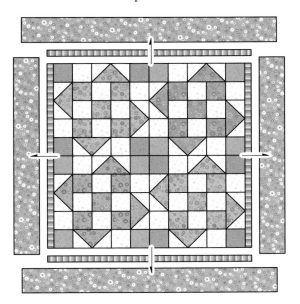

Finishing

Refer to the quilt finishing techniques on pages 72–76 for detailed instructions if needed.

1. Piece the quilt backing (if necessary) so that it is approximately 4" wider and longer than the quilt top. Mark the quilt top if necessary.

2. Layer the quilt top with batting and backing, and baste the layers together. Hand or machine quilt as desired.

3. Trim the batting and backing even with the edges of the quilt top. Add a hanging sleeve if desired. Using the 2¼"-wide green floral strips, prepare the binding and sew it to the quilt. Make a label and attach it to your quilt.

GROWN-UP QUILT IDEA

Start with a wonderful collection of 1800s reproduction fabrics in lights, mediums, and darks. Use the lights and mediums for the block backgrounds, and use the mediums and darks for the other pieces for a truly old-fashioned look. Make 20 blocks and set them in 5 rows of 4 blocks each. Finish your quilt with binding without adding borders to complete that 1800s style.

Sweet Rosebuds

By Laurie Bevan. Quilted by Virginia Lauth, Shoreline, Washington.
- **Quilt Size:** 48½" x 48½"
- **Block Size:** 16" x 16"
- **Block Name:** The Rosebud

This lovely quilt is the perfect gift for a sweet baby girl. By setting the five blocks on point, this became a somewhat larger quilt. The rosebud quilt looks so delicate that I chose to have it hand quilted, and I am grateful to Virginia for her beautiful stitching.

Materials

Yardage is based on 42"-wide fabric.

- ◆ 2½ yards of white print for background
- ◆ ⅜ yard of medium pink print for blocks
- ◆ ⅜ yard of green print for blocks
- ◆ ¼ yard of dark pink mottled fabric for blocks
- ◆ ⅝ yard of green-and-pink stripe for binding
- ◆ 3 yards of fabric for backing
- ◆ 53" x 53" piece of batting

Cutting

All measurements include ¼"-wide seam allowances. Instructions are for cutting strips across the fabric width.

From the dark pink mottled fabric, cut:
2 strips, 2½" x 42"; crosscut into 20 squares, 2½" x 2½"

From the medium pink print, cut:
4 strips, 2½" x 42"; crosscut into:
    60 squares, 2½"x 2½" *or* 20 squares, 2½" x 2½", and 20 rectangles, 2½" x 4½"*

From the green print, cut:
4 strips, 2½" x 42"

From the white print, cut:
1 square, 27" x 27"; cut twice diagonally to yield 4 side triangles

2 squares, 14" x 14"; cut once diagonally to yield 4 corner triangles

5 squares, 8½" x 8½"

2 strips, 4½" x 42"

5 strips, 2½" x 42"; crosscut into 20 pieces, 2½" x 8½"

2 strips, 1½" x 42"; crosscut into 4 pieces, 1½" x 16½"

From the green-and-pink stripe, cut:
2¼"-wide bias strips to equal 206" in length

See step 1 of "Making the Quilt Top." You can piece two squares together or use the 4½"-long rectangles instead. I pieced squares together to make a four patch in the quilt shown.

Making the Quilt Top

After each sewing step, press the seam allowances as directed by the arrows in the illustration.

1. Sew a dark pink square to 20 medium pink squares. Then sew the remaining medium pink squares together in pairs (or replace this unit with the 2½" x 4½" medium pink rectangles). Sew the units together as shown.

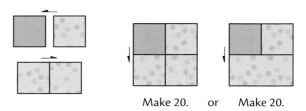

Make 20.   or   Make 20.

2. Sew a green strip to each side of a 4½"-wide white strip. Make two strip sets and cut 20 segments, 2½" wide.

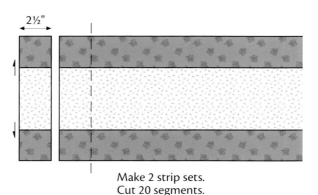

2½"

Make 2 strip sets.
Cut 20 segments.

3. Sew a segment from step 2 to each 2½" x 8½" white piece.

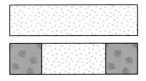 

Make 20.

4. Sew a four-patch unit from step 1 to each end of 10 units from step 3 as shown.

Make 10.

5. Sew the remaining units from step 3, the units from step 4, and the 8½" white squares together as shown. Make five blocks.

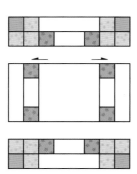 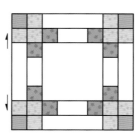

Make 5.

6. Sew a 16½"-long white piece to one side of four of the blocks.

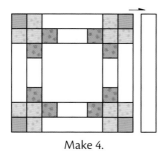

Make 4.

7. Lay out the pieced blocks and the side and corner triangles as shown. Sew the blocks and side triangles together in rows and then sew the rows together. Add the corner triangles last.

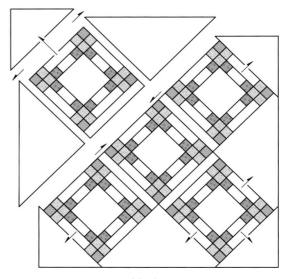

Assembly diagram

8. Trim the edges of the quilt top, leaving 1" of white print beyond the block points. Square up the four corners. The rosebud blocks will appear to float on the background.

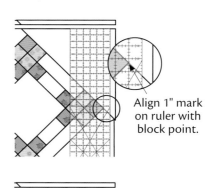

Align 1" mark on ruler with block point.

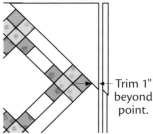

Trim 1" beyond point.

Finishing

Refer to the quilt finishing techniques on pages 72–76 for detailed instructions if needed.

1. Piece the quilt backing (if necessary) so that it is approximately 4" wider and longer than the quilt top. Mark the quilt top if necessary.

2. Layer the quilt top with batting and backing, and baste the layers together. Hand or machine quilt as desired.

3. Trim the batting and backing even with the edges of the quilt top. Add a hanging sleeve if desired. Using the 2¼"-wide green-and-pink bias strips, prepare the binding and sew it to the quilt. Make a label and attach it to your quilt.

Floral quilting designs in the open areas complement the rosebuds perfectly.

Baby Elephant

By Laurie Bevan. Quilted by Dawn Kelly, Ponderay, Idaho.
• **Quilt Size:** 43½" x 52½"
• **Block Size:** 27" x 36"
• **Block Name:** Ararat (variation)

I changed the traditional Ararat block ever so slightly to make this wonderful elephant look like a baby. Polka dots are "in" and readily available, so why not use them as often as possible? They're ideal for a baby elephant. This colorful quilt will brighten any little one's room.

Materials

Yardage is based on 42"-wide fabric.

- ♦ 1⅓ yards of red-with-yellow dot for elephant and binding
- ♦ 1 yard of elephant print for outer border
- ♦ ¾ yard of white dot for background
- ♦ ⅓ yard of blue dot for elephant and inner border
- ♦ ¼ yard of yellow dot for elephant and border corners
- ♦ 2¾ yards of fabric for backing
- ♦ 48" x 57" piece of batting

Cutting

All measurements include ¼"-wide seam allowances. Instructions are for cutting strips across the fabric width.

From the red-with-yellow dot, cut:
1 strip, 9½" x 42"; crosscut into:
 1 piece, 9½" x 24½"
 1 piece, 9½" x 15½"
1 strip, 6½" x 42"; crosscut into:
 3 squares, 6½" x 6½"
 2 rectangles, 3½" x 6½"

 From the remainder of the strip, cut 1 square, 3⅞" x 3⅞"

1 strip, 3⅞" x 42"; crosscut into 10 squares, 3⅞" x 3⅞"

1 strip, 3½" x 42"; crosscut into:
 1 rectangle, 3½" x 9½"
 5 squares, 3½" x 3½"
6 strips, 2¼" x 42"

From the white dot, cut:
1 strip, 6½" x 42"; crosscut into:
 1 rectangle, 6½" x 9½"
 4 rectangles, 3½" x 6½"

1 strip, 3⅞" x 42"; crosscut into 6 squares, 3⅞" x 3⅞"

1 strip, 3½" x 42"; crosscut into:
 1 piece, 3½" x 15½"
 1 piece, 3½" x 12½"
 3 squares, 3½" x 3½"

4 strips, 2" x 42"

From the blue dot, cut:
1 strip, 3⅞" x 42"; crosscut into 3 squares, 3⅞" x 3⅞"

4 strips, 1" x 42"

From the yellow dot, cut:
1 strip, 6½" x 42"; crosscut into:
 4 squares, 6½" x 6½"

 From the remainder of the strip, cut 2 squares, 3⅞" x 3⅞"

From the elephant print, cut:
4 strips, 6½" x 42"

Making the Block

After sewing each step, press the seam allowances as directed by the arrows in the illustration.

1. Draw a diagonal line on the wrong side of the 3⅞" red-with-yellow squares. Place 6 of the squares right sides together with the 3⅞" white squares. Sew ¼" from each side of the drawn line. Cut the squares apart on the line and press. You will use 11 of these triangle squares for the elephant units. Using 3 of the marked squares and the 3 blue squares, make triangle squares for the hoof and eye units. You will need 5 units. Using 2 of the marked squares and the 3⅞" yellow squares, make triangle squares for the ear units. You will need 3 units.

Elephant unit.
Make 11.

Hoof and
eye unit.
Make 5.

Ear unit.
Make 3.

2. Arrange and sew together the following pieces and units to make section A: From the red-with-yellow dot, use one 6½" square, one 3½" x 9½"rectangle, one 3½" x 6½" rectangle, and two 3½" squares. Use two elephant units, one eye unit, and one ear unit from step 1.

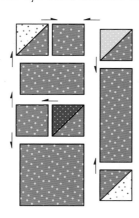 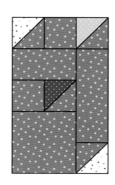

Section A

3. Arrange and sew together the following pieces and units to make section B: From the red-with-yellow dot, use one 3½" square. From the white dot, use one 3½" x 12½" piece, one 3½" x 6½" rectangle, and two 3½" squares. Use three elephant units from step 1.

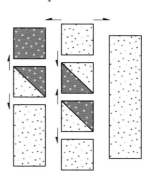 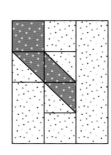

Section B

4. Arrange and sew together the following pieces and units to make section C: From the red-with-yellow dot, use one 9½" x 15½" piece, one 3½" x 6½" rectangle, and two 3½" squares. From the white dot, use one 3½" square. Use two elephant units and two ear units from step 1.

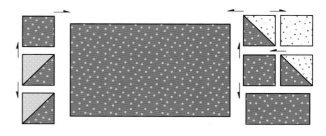

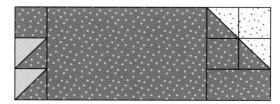

Section C

5. Arrange and sew together the following pieces and units to make section D: From the red-with-yellow dot, use two 6½" squares. From the white dot, use one 6½" x 9½" rectangle and two 3½" x 6½" rectangles. Use two elephant units and four hoof units from step 1.

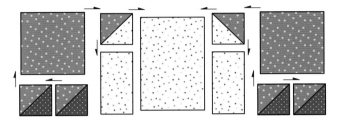

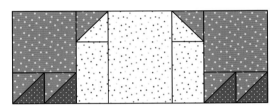

Section D

6. Arrange and sew together the following pieces and units to make section E: From the white dot, use one 3½" x 15½" piece and one 3½" x 6½" rectangle. Use two elephant units from step 1.

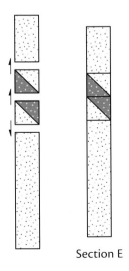

Section E

7. Arrange and sew together sections A through E and the 9½" x 24½" red-with-yellow piece as shown.

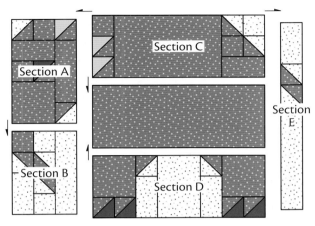

Assembly diagram

Assembling the Quilt Top

1. Trim two of the 2"-wide white strips to a length of 27½". Sew these to the sides of the Elephant block. Trim the remaining two white strips to a length of 39½". Sew these to the top and bottom of the Elephant block.

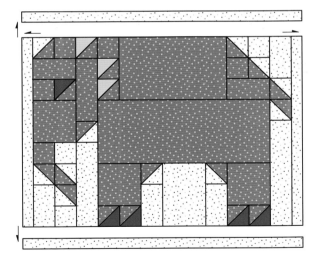

2. Refer to "Adding Borders" on page 71. Attach the 1"-wide blue inner-border strips and the 6½"-wide elephant outer-border strips with the 6½" yellow corner squares to the quilt top. Border lengths should be:

Inner-border strips: 30½" each for sides; 40½" each for top and bottom

Outer-border strips: 31½" each for sides; 40½" each for top and bottom

Add the 6½" corner squares to the top and bottom outer-border strips.

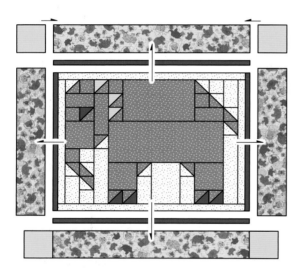

Finishing

Refer to the quilt finishing techniques on pages 72–76 for detailed instructions if needed.

1. Piece the quilt backing (if necessary) so that it is approximately 4" wider and longer than the quilt top. Mark the quilt top if necessary.

2. Layer the quilt top with batting and backing, and baste the layers together. Hand or machine quilt as desired.

3. Trim the batting and backing even with the edges of the quilt top. Add a hanging sleeve if desired. Using the 2¼"-wide red-with-yellow strips, prepare the binding and sew it to the quilt. Make a label and attach it to your quilt.

Outdoor Fun

By Laurie Bevan. Quilted by Karen Ford, Poulsbo, Washington.
- **Quilt Size:** 40½" x 48½"
- **Block Size:** 8" x 12"
- **Block Name:** The World Fair Quilt

Two fabrics, plus one for the binding, are all it takes to make this super-simple and fast baby quilt. Choose a special print to make this quilt for the special baby in your life. The only problem will be narrowing down your choices from all the fabulous juvenile prints that quilt shops carry.

Materials

Yardage is based on 42"-wide fabric.

+ 2 yards of bear print for blocks
+ 1⅜ yards of beige dot for blocks
+ ½ yard of red dot for binding
+ 2½ yards of fabric for backing
+ 45" x 53" piece of batting

Cutting

All measurements include ¼"-wide seam allowances. Instructions are for cutting strips across the fabric width.

From the beige dot, cut:
10 strips, 4½" x 42"; crosscut into 80 squares, 4½" x 4½"

From the bear print, cut:
20 rectangles, 8½" x 12½"

From the red dot, cut:
5 strips, 2¼" x 42"

Making the Quilt Top

After each sewing step, press the seam allowances as directed by the arrows in the illustration.

1. Draw a diagonal line on the wrong side of each beige square. With right sides together, place a marked square on one corner of a bear rectangle and sew on the line. Trim ¼" from the stitched line and press. Repeat to sew a marked square to all four corners of each bear rectangle.

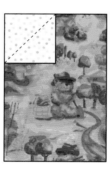

Make 20.

2. Arrange the bear blocks into four rows of five blocks each. Sew the blocks into rows and then sew the rows together. There is a lot of bulk when matching the block seams, so it is best to press the seams open.

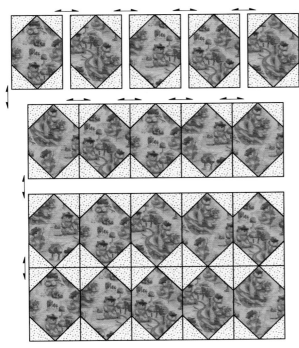

Assembly diagram

Finishing

Refer to the quilt finishing techniques on pages 72–76 for detailed instructions if needed.

1. Piece the quilt backing (if necessary) so that it is approximately 4" wider and longer than the quilt top. Mark the quilt top if necessary.

2. Layer the quilt top with batting and backing, and baste the layers together. Hand or machine quilt as desired.

3. Trim the batting and backing even with the edges of the quilt top. Add a hanging sleeve if desired. Using the 2¼"-wide red strips, prepare the binding and sew it to the quilt. Make a label and attach it to your quilt.

GROWN-UP QUILT IDEA

Try using a selection of Asian prints in place of the bear print. Replace the beige dot corner pieces with two coordinating fabric colors. Use the same color on opposite corners, and when you sew the blocks together, you'll have a two-color diamond between four blocks. Add an inner border of another coordinating color and an outer border of one of your Asian prints, and you've just made a gorgeous, lap-sized quilt.

Baskets for Baby ♥

By Laurie Bevan. Quilted by Dawn Kelly, Ponderay, Idaho.
- **Quilt Size:** 44½" x 44½"
- **Block Size:** 16" x 16"
- **Block Name:** Baby Bunting

Of course, I just had to include the Baby Bunting block in this book. For this quilt, I suggest that you choose a border fabric first; then pick four fabrics that coordinate well with it for the remaining pieces. Have fun with it. You could also set the blocks so that they all face toward the center for a different look.

Materials

Yardage is based on 42"-wide fabric.

- 1 yard of floral print for blocks and outer border
- ⅞ yard of white print for blocks
- ¾ yard of pink print for blocks, border-corner squares, and binding
- ⅜ yard of green print for blocks and inner border
- ¼ yard of yellow print for blocks
- 2¾ yards of fabric for backing
- 49" x 49" piece of batting

Cutting

All measurements include ¼"-wide seam allowances. Instructions are for cutting strips across the fabric width.

From the yellow print, cut:
1 strip, 4½" x 42"

From the green print, cut:
1 strip, 4½" x 42"
4 strips, 1½" x 42"

From the floral print, cut:
4 strips, 5½" x 42"
2 strips, 4½" x 42"; crosscut into 16 squares, 4½" x 4½"

From the white print, cut:
4 strips, 4½" x 42"; crosscut into:
    16 rectangles, 4½" x 8½"
    4 squares, 4½" x 4½"
2 squares, 8⅞" x 8⅞"; cut once diagonally to yield 4 triangles

From the pink print, cut:
1 strip, 4⅞" x 42"; crosscut into 4 squares, 4⅞" x 4⅞". Cut each square once diagonally to yield 8 triangles.
1 strip, 5½" x 42"; crosscut into 4 squares, 5½" x 5½"
5 strips, 2¼" x 42"

Making the Blocks

After each sewing step, press the seam allowances as directed by the arrows in the illustration.

1. Sew together the 4½"-wide yellow and green strips along the strip length. Crosscut the strip set into eight segments, 4½" long. Sew pairs of segments together to make four-patch units as shown.

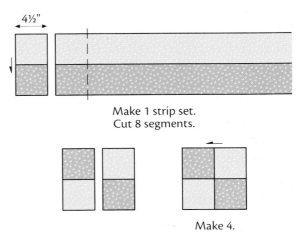

Make 1 strip set.
Cut 8 segments.

Make 4.

2. Draw a diagonal line on the wrong side of the floral squares. With right sides together, place a square at one end of a white rectangle. Sew on the diagonal line. Trim ¼" from the stitched line and press. Place another square at the opposite end of each rectangle. Be sure the diagonal line is oriented in the opposite direction of the first square. Sew, trim, and press as before.

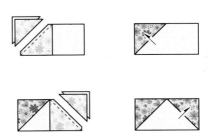

Make 8.

3. Arrange and sew together the units from steps 1 and 2 and the white squares to make the upper basket.

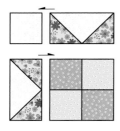 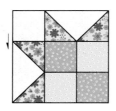

Make 4.

4. Sew a pink triangle to one end of each of the remaining white rectangles, positioning the triangles as shown to make four of each basket-foot unit.

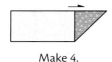 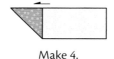

Make 4.   Make 4.

5. Sew the appropriate basket-foot unit to the lower edge of each upper basket as shown. Sew the remaining basket-foot units to the right side.

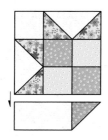 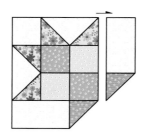

6. Fold each white triangle in half along the long edge and finger-press. With right sides together, center the crease over the bottom point of the basket section. Sew the seam and press. Trim any dog-ears.

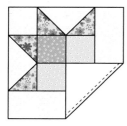 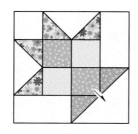

Make 4.

Assembling the Quilt Top

1. Arrange and sew together the four blocks as shown.

2. Referring to "Adding Borders" on page 71 for additional instructions, attach the 1½"-wide green inner-border strips and the 5½"-wide floral outer-border strips with the 5½" pink corner squares to the quilt top. Border lengths should be:

   Inner-border strips: 32½" each for sides; 34½" each for top and bottom
   Outer-border strips: 34½" each for sides, top, and bottom

Add the 5½" pink squares to the top and bottom outer-border strips.

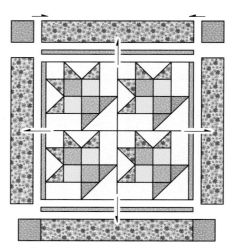

Finishing

Refer to the quilt finishing techniques on pages 72–76 for detailed instructions if needed.

1. Piece the quilt backing (if necessary) so that it is approximately 4" wider and longer than the quilt top. Mark the quilt top if necessary.

2. Layer the quilt top with batting and backing, and baste the layers together. Hand or machine quilt as desired.

3. Trim the batting and backing even with the edges of the quilt top. Add a hanging sleeve if desired. Using the 2¼"-wide pink strips, prepare the binding and sew it to the quilt. Make a label and attach it to your quilt.

Double Dutch ▶▶

Designed by Laurie Bevan. Pieced by Laura Roberts, Lafayette, Colorado.
Quilted by Shirley Bowen, Morrison, Colorado.

- Quilt Size: 40½" x 40½"
- Block Size: 24" x 24"
- Block Name: Double Dutch

I like the name of this block because it reminds me of the children's jump-rope game that I played in my younger days. I found the block in Marsha McCloskey's book *Block Party: A Quilter's Extravaganza of 120 Rotary-Cut Block Patterns* (Rodale Inc., 1998). Thanks, Marsha, for letting me use your Double Dutch block to make this darling, single big-block baby quilt.

Materials

Yardage is based on 42"-wide fabric.

- 1¼ yards of turquoise tonal print for block and outer border
- ⅞ yard of pink mottled fabric for block and binding
- ½ yard of green mottled fabric for block
- ½ yard of light pink dot for block and inner border
- 2½ yards of fabric for backing
- 45" x 45" piece of batting

Cutting

All measurements include ¼"-wide seam allowances. Instructions are for cutting strips across the fabric width.

From the light pink dot, cut:
2 strips, 3½" x 42"; crosscut into 16 squares, 3½" x 3½"

4 strips, 2½" x 42"

From the turquoise tonal print, cut:
1 strip, 6⅞" x 42"; crosscut into:
    2 squares, 6⅞" x 6⅞"

    From the remainder of the strip, cut 4 rectangles, 3½" x 6½"

4 strips, 6½" x 42"

From the pink mottled fabric, cut:
2 strips, 6½" x 42"; crosscut into:
    4 rectangles, 6½" x 12½"
    4 rectangles, 3½" x 6½"

5 strips, 2¼" x 42"

From the green mottled fabric, cut:
1 strip, 6⅞" x 42"; crosscut into:
    2 squares, 6⅞" x 6⅞"

    From the remainder of the strip, cut 2 squares, 6½" x 6½"

1 strip, 6½" x 42"; crosscut into 6 squares, 6½" x 6½"

Assembling the Quilt Top

After each sewing step, press the seam allowances as directed by the arrows in the illustration.

1. Draw a diagonal line on the wrong side of each light pink square. With right sides together, place a square at one end of each turquoise rectangle. Sew on the diagonal line. Trim ¼" from the stitched line and press. Place another square at the opposite end of each rectangle. Be sure the diagonal line is oriented in the opposite direction of the first square. Sew, trim, and press as before. Make four of these flying-geese units. Repeat this step, using the remaining light pink squares and the small pink mottled rectangles. Make four of these flying-geese units.

              Make 4.   Make 4.

2. Repeat step 1, using the 6½" green squares and the large pink mottled rectangles. Make four of these flying-geese units.

Make 4.

3. Draw a diagonal line on the wrong side of each 6⅞" green square. Place each square right sides together with a turquoise square. Sew ¼" from each side of the drawn line. Cut on the line and press. Make four triangle squares.

Make 4.

4. Arrange and sew together one large flying-geese unit, one of each color small flying-geese unit, and one triangle square as shown. Repeat to make a total of four of these sections.

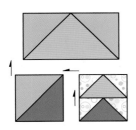 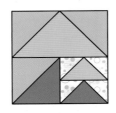

Make 4.

5. Arrange the four sections as shown. Sew them together in pairs and then sew the pairs together to make the Double Dutch block.

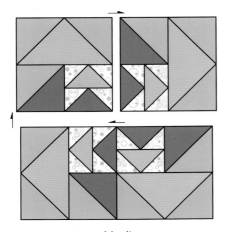

Assembly diagram

6. Referring to "Adding Borders" on page 71, attach the 2½"-wide light pink inner-border strips and the 6½"-wide turquoise outer-border strips to the quilt top. Border lengths should be:
   Inner-border strips: 24½" each for sides; 28½" each for top and bottom
   Outer-border strips: 28½" each for sides; 40½" each for top and bottom

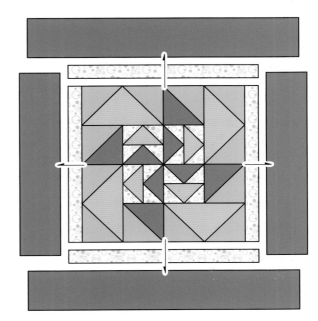

Finishing

Refer to the quilt finishing techniques on pages 72–76 for detailed instructions if needed.

1. Piece the quilt backing (if necessary) so that it is approximately 4" wider and longer than the quilt top. Mark the quilt top if necessary.

2. Layer the quilt top with batting and backing, and baste the layers together. Hand or machine quilt as desired.

3. Trim the batting and backing even with the edges of the quilt top. Add a hanging sleeve if desired. Using the 2¼"-wide pink mottled strips, prepare the binding and sew it to the quilt. Make a label and attach it to your quilt.

Waddlin' Around

By Laurie Bevan. Quilted by Ann Jones, Poulsbo, Washington.
• Quilt Size: 46½" x 46½"
• Block Size: 15" x 15"
• Block Name: Grandma's Hopscotch

I just had to have this ducky print, and then it took three quilt shops to find just the right yellows and oranges to go with it! The ducks waddled across the grain, so I was unable to cut lengthwise strips for the top and bottom borders, and I had to piece them. Show me the baby who's going to notice.

Materials

Yardage is based on 42"-wide fabric.

+ 1¼ yards of ducky print for outer border
+ ⅝ yard of yellow dot for blocks
+ ½ yard of orange-and-yellow stripe for blocks
+ ½ yard of orange swirl for blocks
+ ¼ yard of orange with pink dots for inner border
+ ⅜ yard of teal tonal print for binding
+ 2⅞ yards of fabric for backing
+ 51" x 51" piece of batting

Cutting

All measurements include ¼"-wide seam allowances. Instructions are for cutting strips across the fabric width.

From the yellow dot, cut:
2 strips, 6¼" x 42"; crosscut into:
    8 squares, 6¼" x 6¼"; cut twice diagonally to yield 32 triangles
    From the remainder of the strip, cut 2 squares, 5⅞" x 5⅞"

1 strip, 5⅞" x 42"; crosscut into 6 squares, 5⅞" x 5⅞"

From the orange-and-yellow stripe, cut:
1 strip, 5⅞" x 42"; crosscut into 4 squares, 5⅞" x 5⅞"

1 strip, 6¼" x 42"; crosscut into 4 squares, 6¼" x 6¼". Cut squares twice diagonally to yield 16 triangles.

From the orange swirl, cut:
2 strips, 6¼" x 42"; crosscut into:
    8 squares, 6¼" x 6¼"; cut twice diagonally to yield 32 triangles
    From the remainder of the strip, cut 4 squares, 5⅞" x 5⅞"

From the orange with pink dots, cut:
4 strips, 1½" x 42"

From the ducky print, cut:
5 strips, 7½" x 42"

From the teal tonal print, cut:
5 strips, 2¼" x 42"

Making the Blocks

After each sewing step, press the seam allowances as directed by the arrows in the illustration.

1. Draw a diagonal line on the wrong side of each 5⅞" yellow dot square. Place four of the squares right sides together with each of the 5⅞" orange-and-yellow stripe squares. Sew ¼" from each side of the drawn line. Cut the squares apart on the line and press. Place the remaining four yellow squares right sides together with each of the 5⅞" orange swirl squares. Sew, trim, and press as before.

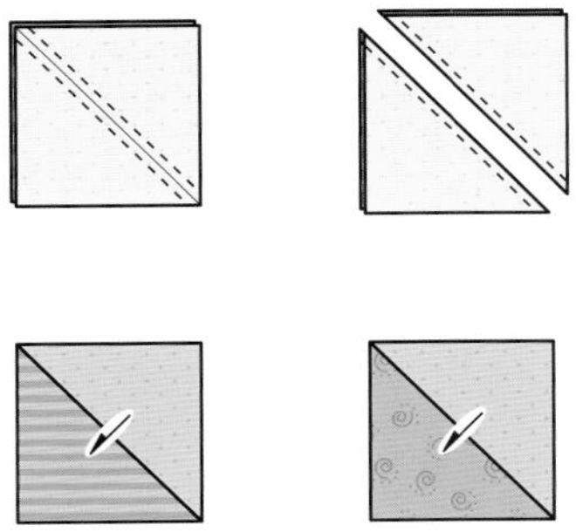

Make 8.   Make 8.

2. Sew the triangle squares from step 1 together as shown to make four center units for the blocks.

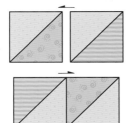 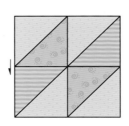

Make 4.

3. Sew 16 of the yellow dot triangles together with the orange swirl triangles as shown to make the side units.

Make 16.

4. Sew the remaining yellow dot triangles together with the orange-and-yellow stripe triangles as shown to make the corner units.

Make 16.

5. Arrange and sew together one center unit from step 2, four side units from step 3, and four corner units from step 4 to make one block. Repeat to make a total of four blocks.

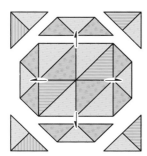 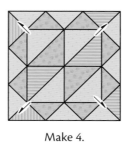

Make 4.

Assembling the Quilt Top

1. Sew the four blocks together as shown.

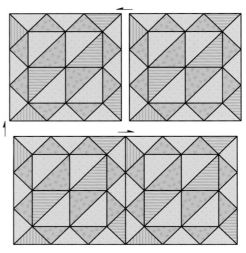

Assembly diagram

2. Referring to "Adding Borders" on page 71, attach the 1½"-wide orange inner-border strips and the 7½"-wide ducky outer-border strips to the quilt top. Border lengths should be:
    Inner-border strips: 30½" each for sides; 32½" each for top and bottom
    Outer-border strips: 32½" each for sides; 46½" each for top and bottom

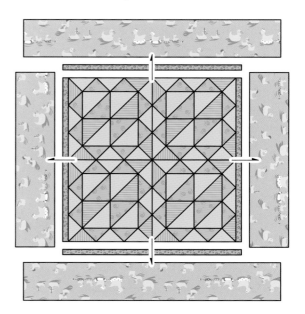

Finishing

Refer to the quilt finishing techniques on pages 72–76 for detailed instructions if needed.

1. Piece the quilt backing (if necessary) so that it is approximately 4" wider and longer than the quilt top. Mark the quilt top if necessary.

2. Layer the quilt top with batting and backing, and baste the layers together. Hand or machine quilt as desired.

3. Trim the batting and backing even with the edges of the quilt top. Add a hanging sleeve if desired. Using the 2¼"-wide teal strips, prepare the binding and sew it to the quilt. Make a label and attach it to your quilt.

GROWN-UP QUILT IDEA

Choose four batik fabrics: a light, a medium, a dark, and something fabulous for the outer border. Use the light in place of the yellow dot, the medium in place of the orange-and-yellow stripe, and the dark in place of the orange swirl. If you make 12 blocks and add an inner border of your dark batik and an outer border of the fabulous batik you chose, you'll have made a beautiful quilt just for yourself.

With Love

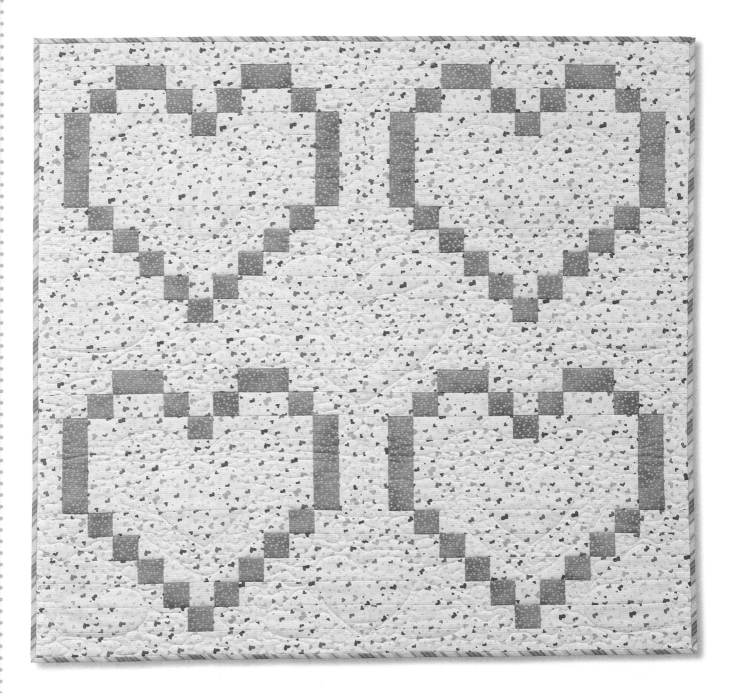

Designed by Laurie Bevan. Pieced by Suzanne Kolhagen, Key West, Florida.
Quilted by Ann Jones, Poulsbo, Washington.
- Quilt Size: 39½" x 39½"
- Block Size: 19½" x 19½"
- Block Name: Pieced Heart

I think this is such a very clever heart block. All you do is sew together strips and squares. Suzanne did a beautiful job of piecing this top, and I'm happy that she likes it as much as I do. But now we have to decide which baby is going to get this one!

Materials

Yardage is based on 42"-wide fabric.
- 1⅝ yards of heart print for background
- ½ yard of pink dot for hearts
- ⅝ yard of pink-and-green stripe for binding
- 2½ yards of fabric for backing
- 44" x 44" piece of batting

Cutting

All measurements include ¼"-wide seam allowances. Instructions are for cutting strips across the fabric width.

From the heart print, cut:
2 strips, 5" x 42"; crosscut into 4 pieces, 5" x 14" (piece A)
20 strips, 2" x 42"; crosscut into:
   8 pieces, 2" x 20" (piece B)
   4 pieces, 2" x 11" (piece C)
   8 pieces, 2" x 9½" (piece D)
   12 pieces, 2" x 8" (piece E)
   24 pieces, 2" x 6½" (piece F)
   24 pieces, 2" x 5" (piece G)
   24 pieces, 2" x 3½" (piece H)
   8 squares, 2" x 2" (piece I)

From the pink dot, cut:
5 strips, 2" x 42"; crosscut into:
   8 pieces, 2" x 6½" (piece J)
   8 pieces, 2" x 3½" (piece K)
   56 squares, 2" x 2" (piece L)

From the pink-and-green stripe, cut:
2¼"-wide bias strips to equal 170" in length

Assembling the Quilt Top

After each sewing step, press the seam allowances as directed by the arrows in the illustration.

1. Arrange and sew together one B piece, three G pieces, two K pieces, four H pieces, four L squares, and one I square as shown to make section 1. Repeat to make a total of four of these sections. Press the horizontal seams up on two sections and down on two sections.

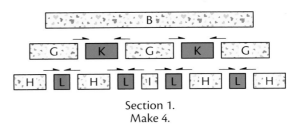

Section 1.
Make 4.

2. Arrange and sew together one A piece, four F pieces, two J pieces, and one L square as shown to make section 2. Repeat to make a total of four of these sections.

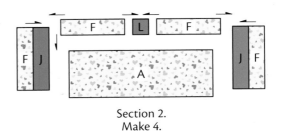

Section 2.
Make 4.

3. Arrange and sew together one C piece, two H pieces, three E pieces, three G pieces, two F pieces, one I square, two D pieces, nine L squares, and one B piece as shown to make

section 3. Repeat to make a total of four of these sections. Press the horizontal seams up on two sections and down on two sections.

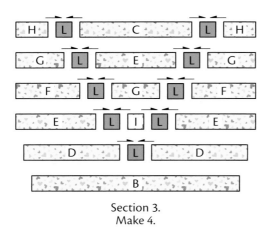

Section 3.
Make 4.

4. Arrange and sew together one section 1, one section 2, and one section 3 as shown to make the Pieced Heart block. Join sections with the seams pressed in the same direction. Make a total of four blocks with horizontal seams pressed down on two blocks and up on two blocks.

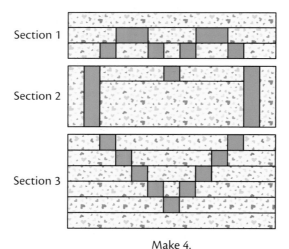

Make 4.

5. Sew the blocks together in pairs as shown, and then sew the pairs together to make the quilt top.

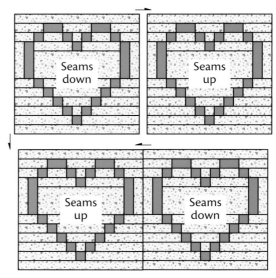

Assembly diagram

Finishing

Refer to the quilt finishing techniques on pages 72–76 for detailed instructions if needed.

1. Piece the quilt backing (if necessary) so that it is approximately 4" wider and longer than the quilt top. Mark the quilt top if necessary.

2. Layer the quilt top with batting and backing, and baste the layers together. Hand or machine quilt as desired.

3. Trim the batting and backing even with the edges of the quilt top. Add a hanging sleeve if desired. Using the 2¼"-wide pink-and-green bias strips, prepare the binding and sew it to the quilt. Make a label and attach it to your quilt.

For More than One

By Laurie Bevan. Quilted by Shirley Bowen, Morrison, Colorado.
• **Quilt Size: 36½" x 42½"**
• **Block Size: 36" x 42"**
• **Block Name: Triplet (variation)**

Is the mother-to-be expecting more than one baby? Then make as many of these quilts as you need, using a different set of fabrics for each one. This is also a terrific pattern to use for charity baby quilts.

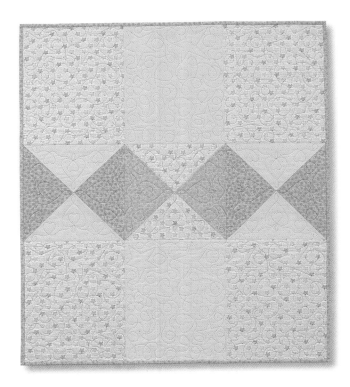

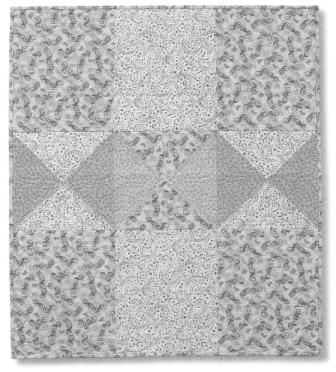

Materials for One Quilt

Yardage is based on 42"-wide fabric.

+ 1¼ yards of yellow heart-print flannel for block
+ 1¼ yards of green print flannel for block and binding
+ ½ yard of pink print flannel for block
+ ½ yard of purple print flannel for block
+ 1½ yards of fabric for backing
+ 41" x 47" piece of batting

Cutting

All measurements include ¼"-wide seam allowances. Instructions are for cutting strips across the fabric width.

From the pink print, cut:
1 square, 14" x 14"

From the green print, cut:
2 rectangles, 12½" x 15½"

1 square, 14" x 14"

5 strips, 2½" x 42"

From the purple print, cut:
1 square, 14" x 14"

From the yellow heart print, cut:
4 rectangles, 12½" x 15½"

1 square, 14" x 14"

Assembling the Quilt Top

After each sewing step, press the seam allowances as directed by the arrows in the illustration.

1. Draw two diagonal lines on the wrong side of the pink square. Place the pink square right sides together with the green square. Beginning at one corner, sew ¼" to the right of that line until you reach the intersecting line. With your needle down on this line, turn the squares 90° and sew on this diagonal line for ½". With your

needle down, rotate the squares back 90° and continue sewing, now with your stitching ¼" to the left of the first line, until you reach the opposite corner. Remove the squares from your machine and sew the other diagonal line in the same manner. Cut along both diagonal lines and press.

 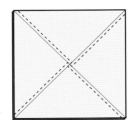

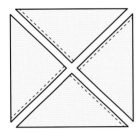 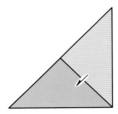

2. Sew the units from step 1 together as shown to make two squares. Press the seams in either direction. Trim these squares to 12½" x 12½". Be sure to center your ruler on the square and align the 45° angle line with the seam line. You want to make sure that the four corners are cut perfectly square.

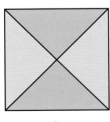

Make 2.

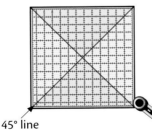

45° line

3. Draw two diagonal lines on the wrong side of the purple square. Place the purple square right sides together with the yellow square. Sew, cut, and press as in step 1. You will use two of the triangle units you made.

4. Sew two units from step 3 together as shown to make a square. Press the seam in either

direction. Trim this square to 12½" x 12½" as you did in step 2.

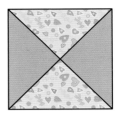

Make 1.

5. Arrange and sew together the four yellow rectangles, the two green rectangles, and the three pieced squares as shown.

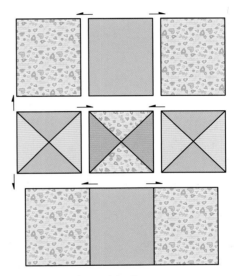

Assembly diagram

Finishing

Refer to the quilt finishing techniques on pages 72–76 for detailed instructions if needed.

1. Piece the quilt backing (if necessary) so that it is approximately 4" wider and longer than the quilt top. Mark the quilt top if necessary.

2. Layer the quilt top with batting and backing, and baste the layers together. Hand or machine quilt as desired.

3. Trim the batting and backing even with the edges of the quilt top. Using the 2½"-wide green strips, prepare the binding and sew it to the quilt. Make a label and attach it to your quilt.

Animal Friends

By Laurie Bevan. Quilted by Karen Ford, Poulsbo, Washington.
- **Quilt Size:** 45½" x 45½"
- **Block Size:** 15" x 15"
- **Block Name:** Web

The Web block is the perfect showcase for a large-scale baby print. Just use the print again in the border to tie the quilt together. This unusual-looking block is easy to sew too.

Materials

Yardage is based on 42"-wide fabric.

+ 1½ yards of animal print for blocks and outer border
+ ¾ yard of blue print for blocks and inner, middle, and outer borders
+ ⅔ yard of pink print for blocks and inner and middle borders
+ ¼ yard of black dot for blocks
+ ¼ yard of white dot for blocks
+ ½ yard of black-and-white print for binding
+ 2⅞ yards of fabric for backing
+ 50" x 50" piece of batting

Cutting

All measurements include ¼"-wide seam allowances. Instructions are for cutting strips across the fabric width unless otherwise specified.

From the animal print, cut:
2 strips, 5½" x 42"

> From the *lengthwise grain* of the remaining animal print, cut:

> 2 strips, 5½" x the length of fabric

> From the remaining animal print, cut:
> 4 squares, 10½" x 10½"

From the pink print, cut:
4 strips, 3" x 42"; crosscut into 16 pieces, 3" x 8½"

4 strips, 2" x 42"

From the blue print, cut:
1 strip, 5½" x 42"; crosscut into 4 squares, 5½" x 5½"

4 strips, 2½" x 42"; crosscut into 16 pieces, 2½" x 8½"

4 strips, 1½" x 42"

From the black dot, cut:
1 strip, 5⅞" x 42"; crosscut into 4 squares, 5⅞" x 5⅞". Cut each square once diagonally to yield 8 triangles.

From the white dot, cut:
1 strip, 5⅞" x 42"; crosscut into 4 squares, 5⅞" x 5⅞". Cut each square once diagonally to yield 8 triangles.

From the black-and-white print, cut:
5 strips, 2¼" x 42"

Making the Blocks

After each sewing step, press the seam allowances as directed by the arrows in the illustration.

1. Make a mark 3" from each corner of the animal-print squares. Draw a diagonal line from point to point across each corner. Cut on each drawn line to create an octagonal block center.

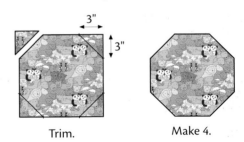

Trim.   Make 4.

2. Sew an 8½"-long pink piece to the top edge of each animal-print octagon, stitching for about 3" and stopping approximately 2" from the corner of the octagon as shown. There is no need to backstitch because you will be sewing over this stitching later. Remove the block from the

machine and press. Trim the completely sewn end of the pink strip even with the edge of the octagon as shown.

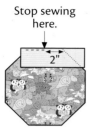 

3. Sew an 8½"-long blue piece to the edge you just trimmed, which means you are adding the strips counterclockwise around the octagon. Press and trim as in step 1.

 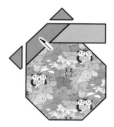

Trim.

4. Continue adding pieces around the octagon, alternating pink and blue, until you reach the last side.

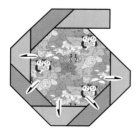

5. Fold back the unsewn end of the pink piece. Sew a blue piece to the final side of the octagon. Press and trim as before.

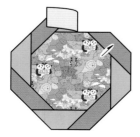

6. Finger-press the unsewn seam allowance of the pink piece so it is flat, and finish sewing this seam, overlapping the previous stitching by ½". Sew to the end of the piece. Press and trim as needed.

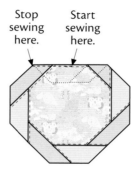 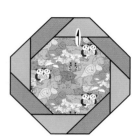

Make 4.

7. Sew two black triangles and two white triangles to opposite corners of each block.

 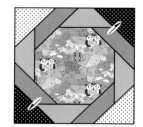

Make 4.

Assembling the Quilt Top

1. Sew the four blocks together as shown.

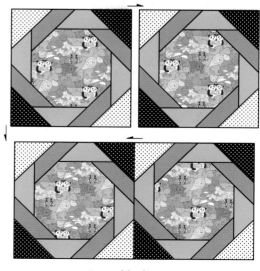

Assembly diagram

2. Refer to "Adding Borders" on page 71 for additional instructions. For the inner border, trim two 2"-wide pink strips to a length of 30½". Sew these to the sides of the quilt top. Trim two 1½"-wide blue strips to a length of 33½". Sew these to the top and bottom of the quilt top.

3. For the middle border, trim two 1½"-wide blue strips to a length of 32½". Sew these to the sides of the quilt top. Trim two 2"-wide pink strips to a length of 35½". Sew these to the top and bottom of the quilt top.

4. For the outer border, trim the 5½"-wide animal-print strips to a length of 35½". Sew two of these strips to the sides of the quilt center. Be sure the animals are facing the same direction as the animals in the block centers. Sew the 5½" blue squares to each end of the two remaining strips as shown. Sew these strips to the top and bottom of the quilt top. Once again, check that the animals are facing the right direction.

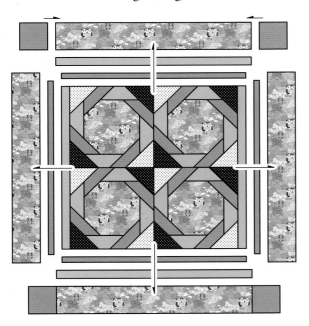

Finishing

Refer to the quilt finishing techniques on pages 72–76 for detailed instructions if needed.

1. Piece the quilt backing (if necessary) so that it is approximately 4" wider and longer than the quilt top. Mark the quilt top if necessary.

2. Layer the quilt top with batting and backing, and baste the layers together. Hand or machine quilt as desired.

3. Trim the batting and backing even with the edges of the quilt top. Add a hanging sleeve if desired. Using the 2¼"-wide black-and-white strips, prepare the binding and sew it to the quilt. Make a label and attach it to your quilt.

The Tin Man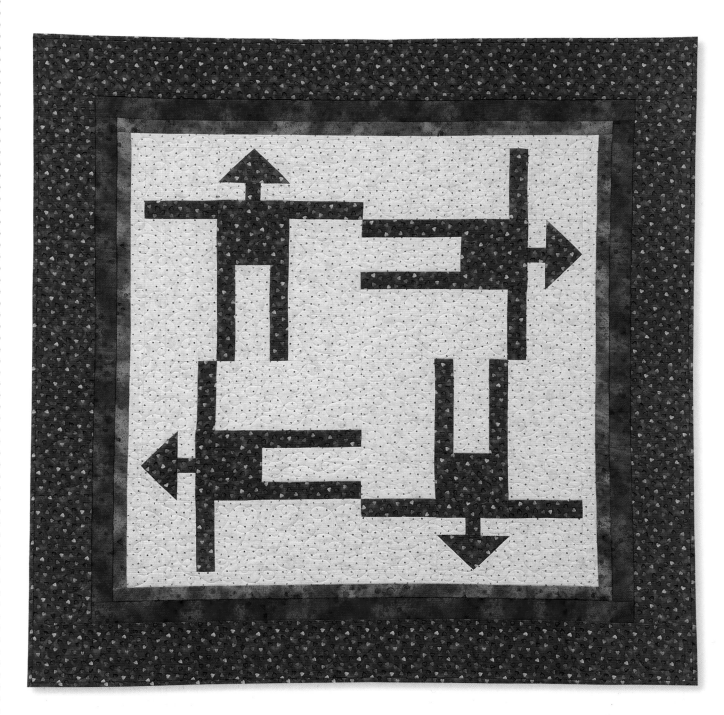

By Laurie Bevan. Quilted by Ann Jones, Poulsbo, Washington.

- **Quilt Size:** 45½" x 45½"
- **Block Size:** 15" x 15"
- **Block Name:** Tin Man

This is a great setting for these four blocks. Turn each block 90° so one block faces each direction. Then quilt a heart on each Tin Man's chest so no trip to see the Wizard will be needed.

Materials

Yardage is based on 42"-wide fabric.

+ 1½ yards of blue heart print for blocks, outer border, and binding
+ 1⅛ yards of beige print for blocks
+ ⅓ yard of mottled red fabric for middle border
+ ¼ yard of mottled green fabric for inner border
+ 2⅞ yards of fabric for backing
+ 50" x 50" piece of batting

Cutting

All measurements include ¼"-wide seam allowances. Instructions are for cutting strips across the fabric width.

From the blue heart print, cut:
1 strip, 5½" x 42"; crosscut into:
    4 rectangles, 5" x 5½"
    4 rectangles, 3" x 5½"
5 strips, 4½" x 42"
5 strips, 2¼" x 42"
3 strips, 1¾" x 42"; crosscut into:
    8 pieces, 1¾" x 7¼"
    8 pieces, 1¾" x 5½"
    4 rectangles, 1½" x 1¾"

From the beige print, cut:
3 strips, 5½" x 42"; crosscut into:
    8 rectangles, 5½" x 10½"
    8 rectangles, 4¼" x 5½"
2 strips, 3" x 42"; crosscut into:
    4 rectangles, 3" x 7¼"
    8 squares, 3" x 3"
1 strip, 1¾" x 42"; crosscut into 8 rectangles, 1¾" x 2½"
4 strips, 1½" x 42"

From the mottled green fabric, cut:
4 strips, 1½" x 42"

From the mottled red fabric, cut:
4 strips, 2" x 42"

Making the Blocks

After each sewing step, press the seam allowances as directed by the arrows in the illustration.

1. Sew a 1¾" x 5½" blue piece between a 4¼" x 5½" beige rectangle and a 5½" x 10½" beige rectangle as shown to make the arm section. Make a total of eight arm sections.

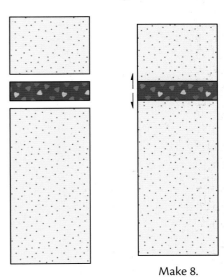

Make 8.

2. Draw a diagonal line on the wrong side of each 3" beige square. With right sides together, place a marked beige square at one end of a 3" x 5½" blue rectangle as shown on the following page. Sew on the drawn line. Trim ¼" from the stitched line and press. Place another beige square at the opposite end of the rectangle. Be sure the diagonal line is oriented in the opposite

direction of the first square. Sew, trim, and press as before to make a head unit. Make a total of four head units.

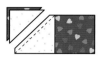
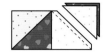

Make 4.

3. Sew a 1½" x 1¾" blue rectangle between two 1¾" x 2½" beige rectangles as shown to make a neck unit. Make a total of four neck units.

Make 4.

4. Sew a 3" x 7¼" beige rectangle between two 1¾" x 7¼" blue pieces as shown to make a leg unit. Make a total of four leg units.

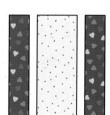

Make 4.

5. Arrange and sew together one head unit, one neck unit, one 5" x 5½" blue heart rectangle, and one leg unit to create the body section. Make a total of four body sections.

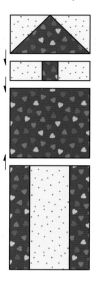
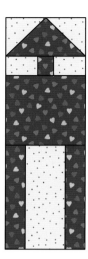

Make 4.

6. Arrange and sew together one body section and two arm sections to make one block. Make a total of four blocks.

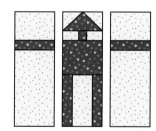
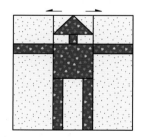

Make 4.

Assembling the Quilt Top

1. Arrange and sew together the four blocks as shown.

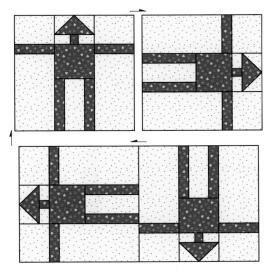

Assembly diagram

2. Trim two of the 1½"-wide beige strips to a length of 30½". Sew these to the sides of the quilt center. Trim the remaining two beige strips to a length of 32½". Sew these to the top and bottom of the quilt top.

3. Referring to "Adding Borders" on page 71, attach the 1½"-wide green inner-border strips, the 2"-wide red middle-border strips, and the 4½"-wide blue print outer-border strips to the quilt top. Border lengths should be:

    Inner-border strips: 32½" each for sides; 34½" each for top and bottom

Middle-border strips: 34½" each for sides; 37½" each for top and bottom

Outer-border strips: 37½" each for sides; 45½" each for top and bottom

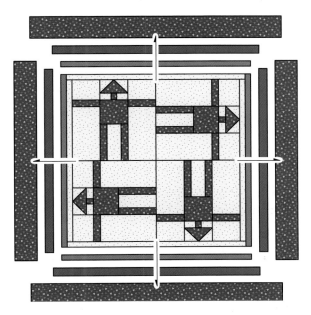

Finishing

Refer to the quilt finishing techniques on pages 72–76 for detailed instructions if needed.

1. Piece the quilt backing (if necessary) so that it is approximately 4" wider and longer than the quilt top. Mark the quilt top if necessary.

2. Layer the quilt top with batting and backing, and baste the layers together. Hand or machine quilt as desired.

3. Trim the batting and backing even with the edges of the quilt top. Add a hanging sleeve if desired. Using the 2¼"-wide blue strips, prepare the binding and sew it to the quilt. Make a label and attach it to your quilt.

Quiltmaking Basics

The project instructions provided in this book assume that you already have a basic knowledge of quiltmaking. The techniques I used for making these quilts are offered on the next few pages. Please refer to this information to learn about a step you are unfamiliar with or to review a technique. I hope you find this information helpful so you will truly enjoy the process of quiltmaking.

Fabrics and Supplies

Fabric: I use only 100%-cotton fabrics of the highest quality I can afford for my quilts. I always wash my fabrics as soon as I get them home to remove any chemicals on the fabric and to be sure the dyes won't run.

Rotary-cutting tools: A cutting mat, a rotary cutter, and a couple of acrylic rulers are the minimum tools required to cut the strips and pieces for the projects in this book. A mat that measures 24" x 36" is great, but one that is 18" x 24" will work fine. Any rotary cutter will do, but a sharp blade is a must. Always keep an extra new blade with your supplies. A long ruler that is 6" x 24" will work for all the projects. A 6" or 8" square ruler is nice to have as well for crosscutting strips into squares and rectangles. For big-block quilts you might want to invest in a 20½" square ruler for squaring up finished blocks.

Sewing machine: A machine in good working order is essential to piece the quilt tops in this book. A straight stitch with even tension and an accurate ¼" seam guide are all you need. If you want to machine quilt your own tops, you will need a walking-foot and/or darning-foot attachment. Some sewing machine models have a built-in walking foot.

Iron and pressing surface: Any iron that has a cotton temperature setting and a steam option is adequate. A firm, flat surface with insulation and a cloth cover, such as an ironing board or pressing pad, are needed as well. A small surface is fine for pressing blocks, but a larger area is desirable for pressing entire rows and yardage before cutting.

Thread: Use good-quality, 100%-cotton thread for piecing your quilt tops. White, beige, gray, and black are four colors to definitely have on hand. With these four colors, you can piece just about anything. Use cotton thread in a color that matches your binding fabric when hand stitching the binding to the back of your quilt.

Needles: Use a size 70/10 or 80/12 sewing-machine needle for piecing your quilt tops. Change your needle after each major project for best stitch results. A size 90/14 needle is used for machine quilting. Short, sharp hand-sewing needles called Betweens are designed for hand quilting. A standard hand-sewing needle is used for stitching the binding to the backing.

Pins: I prefer long, fine pins with heads for my piecing. The finer the pin, the flatter your layers will lie. Pins with heads are easier to remove, easier to see when your needle reaches them, and certainly faster to find on the floor.

Scissors: A must for your basic supplies is a good, sharp pair of large scissors used only for cutting fabric. A small pair of scissors next to your sewing machine is great for snipping threads.

Seam ripper: This is an extremely valuable tool that is used to remove stitches from incorrectly sewn seams.

Marking tools: You will want to have a sharp lead pencil, a white chalk pencil, and a very fine black fabric marker on hand for drawing lines on the wrong side of fabrics for some of the piecing techniques in this book. Lead pencils, chalk pencils, or special pens can be used for marking quilting designs. Before marking your top, test the tool on your fabric to be sure you can remove the marks easily.

Rotary Cutting

All of the strips and pieces for the projects in this book were rotary cut. If you have never used a rotary cutter for making quilts, please read through these basic directions. For a more thorough lesson, see *The Quilter's Quick Reference Guide* by Candace Eisner Strick (Martingale & Company, 2004). Remember: Always measure twice and cut once!

Cutting Crosswise Strips

1. Fold your fabric in half along the lengthwise grain, matching selvages. With the fold closest to you, place your fabric along the bottom horizontal line of your cutting mat. Be sure your fabric lies flat. Use your long ruler and align one of the vertical lines on the ruler with a vertical line on your mat so that the ruler completely covers both cut ends of the fabric. Cut along the right side of the ruler and discard the uneven scrap.

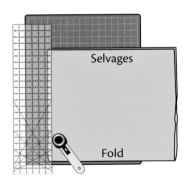

2. To cut the strips, align the correct vertical measurement line on your ruler with the previously cut edge of the fabric. Cut the strip along the right side of the ruler. Cut as many fabric strips as needed. (Reverse the procedure in steps 1 and 2 if you are a left-handed quilter.)

Cutting Lengthwise Strips

1. Fold the length of fabric in half along the crosswise grain, matching selvage edges. Fold the fabric in half again along the crosswise grain, again matching the selvage edges. With the double fold closest to you, place your fabric along the bottom horizontal line of your cutting mat. Be sure your fabric lies flat. Use a long ruler and align one of the vertical lines on the ruler with a vertical line on your mat so that the ruler completely covers the left selvage edge of the fabric. Cut along the right side of the ruler and discard the selvage.

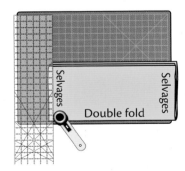

2. To cut the strips, align the correct vertical measurement line on your ruler with the previously cut edge of the fabric. Cut the strip along the right side of the ruler. Continue and

cut as many fabric strips as needed. (Reverse the procedure in steps 1 and 2 if you are a left-handed quilter.)

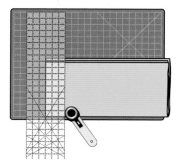

Cutting Squares and Rectangles

Lay the strips that have been cut to the required width on your cutting mat. You may stack strips up to six layers thick to cut many squares or rectangles of the same size. Use your ruler as in step 1 of "Cutting Lengthwise Strips" on page 69 to trim the selvage ends from the strips. Align the left edge (right edge for left-handed quilters) of the strips with the correct ruler marking.

For squares, the length you cut will be the same as the width of the strip.

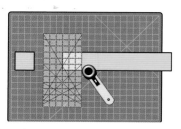

For rectangles, the length you cut will be the measurement of the rectangle (length or width) that is not the width of the strip. For example, if the strip width is 2½", then the length you cut will be 4½" to make a 2½" x 4½" rectangle. If the strip width is 4½", then the length you cut will be 2½".

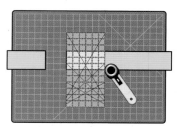 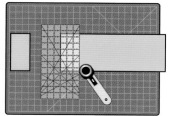

Cutting Squares Diagonally

Align the right edge of your ruler diagonally from corner to corner on each square and cut. You may stack squares up to six layers thick to cut several squares at once. (Align the left edge of your ruler diagonally from corner to corner if you are a left-handed quilter.)

 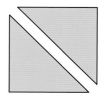

To cut squares twice diagonally, do not disturb the pieces just cut. Align the right edge of your ruler diagonally from one remaining uncut corner to the other uncut corner. Make the second cut.

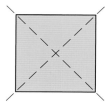 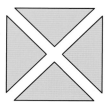

Machine Piecing

A stitched seam with even tension and an accurate ¼"-wide seam allowance are two of the most important requirements for quality machine piecing. Follow the instructions in your sewing-machine manual to properly adjust your thread tension. Some machines have a ¼" foot you can attach and then align your pieces with the edge of the foot as a guide. If you do not have this foot, you can measure ¼" from your needle and use a piece of blue painter's tape or moleskin on your throat plate as a guide.

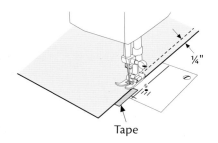

Tape

Chain Piecing

This timesaving technique allows you to save thread and piece many units at once.

1. Start with a small scrap of fabric and sew across it, stopping at the end of the fabric.

2. Feed the unit to be sewn under the presser foot until it almost butts up to the scrap. Sew the seam across this unit, stopping at the end.

3. Continue feeding all the units to be sewn through the machine without cutting the thread between them.

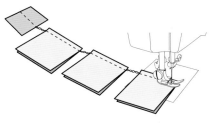

Chain piecing

4. When all the units are sewn, remove the chain from the machine and clip the threads between the units.

Easing

When two pieces to be sewn together differ in size by no more than $\frac{1}{8}$", it is possible to make them fit together. Pin the ends and any intersections that should match; then pin in between to spread the excess fabric evenly. Sew the seam, placing the larger piece on the bottom. The feed dogs will ease the two pieces together.

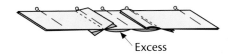

Excess

Pressing

I like to use just a hint of steam when piecing. I believe it makes the seams lie flatter, but be careful as it can also distort the shape of your piece. Be sure to *press* the seam, lifting the iron up and down, rather than using a back-and-forth ironing motion.

Press each seam on the wrong side first to "set" the seam. Then press the seam from the right side in the direction of the pressing arrow on the illustration. Follow the pressing arrows so that when you sew two seamed units together the seams will be pressed in the opposite directions. This allows the seams to butt together and make a perfectly matched intersection.

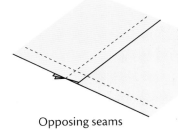

Opposing seams

Adding Borders

When all of your blocks are complete and sewn together as directed in the project instructions, you are ready to add borders. The border-strip lengths given in the project instructions are based on the dimensions of the pieces after sewing an accurate $\frac{1}{4}$"-wide seam allowance. As each quilter's seam allowance may vary slightly, be sure to measure your quilt top as directed below to cut your border strips the length you need.

Borders with Straight-Cut Corners

1. Measure the length of the quilt top through the center. Cut two side border strips this length, piecing as necessary. Mark the centers of the quilt edges and border strips. Pin the borders to the quilt top, matching centers and raw edges. Pin as necessary to make the two pieces ease together. Sew the border strips to the quilt top and press the seam allowances toward the borders.

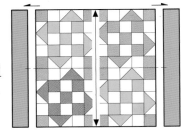

Measure center of quilt, top to bottom. Mark centers.

2. Measure the width of the quilt top through the center, including the side borders you just added. Cut a top and bottom border strip this length, piecing as necessary. Mark the centers of the quilt edges and the border strips. Pin the borders to the quilt top, matching centers and raw edges. Pin as necessary to make the two pieces ease together. Sew the border strips to the quilt top and press the seam allowances toward the borders.

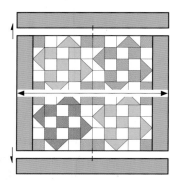

Measure center of quilt, side to side, including border strips. Mark centers.

Borders with Corner Squares

1. Measure the width and length of the quilt top through the center. Cut border strips to those measurements, piecing as necessary. Mark the centers of the quilt edges and the border strips. Pin the side border strips to opposite sides of the quilt top, matching centers and raw edges. Pin as necessary to make the two pieces ease together. Sew the side border strips to the quilt top and press the seam allowances toward the border strips.

2. Cut corner squares of the required size, or piece them as instructed in the project. Sew a corner square to each end of the remaining two border strips and press the seam allowances toward the border strips. Mark the centers of the quilt edges and the border strips. Pin the border strips to the top and bottom edges of the quilt top. Match the centers, the seams between the

border strips and corner squares, and ends. Ease as necessary and stitch. Press the seam allowances toward the border strips.

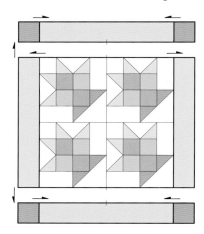

Preparing to Quilt

You have several choices for quilting your project. You may quilt by hand, quilt by machine on your own sewing machine, or hire a professional machine quilter. If you choose to use a professional machine quilter, be sure to ask how to prepare the quilt. If you need to mark quilting designs on your top, it's easier to mark before layering and basting.

Layering and Basting

It is now time to make the quilt "sandwich"—the layers of backing, batting, and quilt top. Your backing fabric should be at least 4" longer and wider then your quilt top.

1. Lay out your backing, wrong side up, on a flat surface and tape or pin the edges to keep it taut. Be careful not to stretch it out of shape.

2. Center the batting on top of the backing and smooth out any wrinkles.

3. Center your pressed quilt top, right side up, on the batting. Be sure the edges of the top are parallel to the edges of the backing. Smooth out any wrinkles until the top is completely flat.

4. If you will be hand quilting, baste using a needle and thread. Start in the center of the quilt top and baste diagonally toward each corner. Next,

baste a grid of horizontal and vertical lines 6" to 8" apart. Finally, baste around the edges.

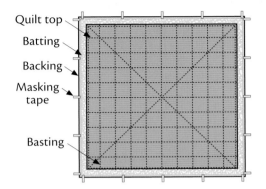

Quilt top
Batting
Backing
Masking tape
Basting

If you will be machine quilting, use large, rust-proof safety pins. Place them about 6" to 8" apart and away from the places where you plan to quilt.

Quilting

Most of the quilts in this book were machine quilted by talented professionals, and one was hand quilted by a good friend. If you would like to do the quilting yourself by hand or machine, refer to one of the many good books on the subject, or take a class at a local quilt shop if you need assistance.

Adding a Hanging Sleeve

If you plan to hang your quilt on a wall, you will need to sew a sleeve on the back for a rod or dowel before binding.

1. Cut a piece of backing fabric (or muslin) 6" to 8" wide and 1" shorter than the width of your quilt. Fold the short ends under ½" and then another ½" to create a hem. Press the folds to keep the hem flat, and sew ⅜" from each edge.

2. Fold the fabric in half lengthwise, wrong sides together. Align the raw edges with the top of the quilt on the backing side and machine baste across the top. When you sew the binding on, the sleeve will be firmly attached to the quilt.

Sleeve

Quilt back

3. After the binding has been sewn on, blindstitch the bottom of the sleeve to the quilt backing. Raise the bottom edge of the sleeve up a bit to provide a little room so the hanging rod does not put strain on the quilt.

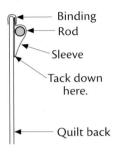

Binding
Rod
Sleeve
Tack down here.
Quilt back

Binding

Even though I rarely do the quilting on my own quilts, I always add the binding myself. I like to be the last person to work on the quilt. After machine sewing the binding to the front, it is a pleasure to sit and hand stitch the binding to the back. I watch a favorite movie while I stitch, and I'm done in no time.

Cutting Straight-Grain Binding

I generally cut binding strips across the width of the fabric 2¼" wide. For flannel, I cut 2½"-wide strips because you need the extra width to bind the thicker flannel layers. Follow the cutting instructions for each project and cut the number of strips needed from your binding fabric.

Cutting Bias Binding

When using a plaid or stripe, I often cut the strips on the bias for a nice accent.

1. Align the 45° line of a square ruler along the selvage and place a long ruler against it. Cut along the edge of the long ruler.

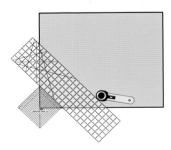

2. Align the 2¼" or 2½" line on the ruler (width of the binding strip) with the previously cut edge of the fabric. Cut along the edge of the ruler. Continue cutting strips until your ruler is not long enough to completely reach across the entire piece of fabric.

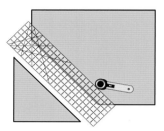

3. Carefully fold the fabric toward you as shown. Be sure the bias edges are aligned. Continue to cut bias strips until you have enough to make the required length of binding.

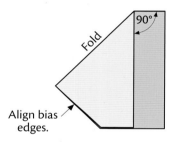

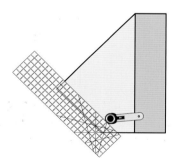

Attaching the Binding

1. Join *straight-grain binding strips*, right sides together, at right angles by sewing on the diagonal from corner to corner as shown. Join *bias-cut binding strips* with right sides together and the diagonal edges aligned; sew across the strips as shown. Trim the excess fabric and press

the seams open. Continue joining strips until you have one long strip of binding.

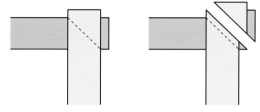

Joining straight-grain strips

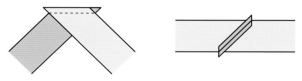

Joining bias-cut strips

2. Fold the long strip in half lengthwise, wrong sides together, and press.

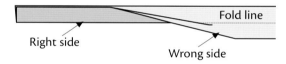

3. Trim the batting and backing even with the edges of the quilt top. Now is the time to add a hanging sleeve if you need one. See "Adding a Hanging Sleeve" on page 73 for instructions.

4. Use a walking foot and a slightly longer stitch to sew the binding to the quilt. Align the raw edges of the binding strip with the front edge of the quilt top and start sewing near the middle of one side of the quilt, using a ¼"-wide seam allowance. Leave at least the first 6" of the binding strip unsewn to finish the binding at the end. Stop sewing ¼" from the corner of the quilt.

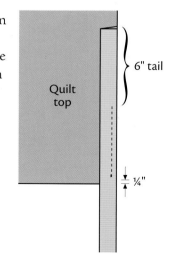

5. Remove the needle from the quilt and turn the quilt so you will be sewing down the next side. Fold the binding up, away from the quilt, with raw edges aligned. Fold the binding back down onto itself, even with the edge of the quilt top. Start sewing ¼" from the corner and backstitch a few stitches. Then sew forward down the second side of the quilt. Stop sewing when you are ¼" from the corner and repeat the process to sew around all sides of the quilt.

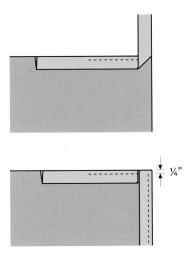

6. When you are again sewing on the side where you started, stop sewing approximately 7" from where you began. Overlap the beginning tail with the ending tail. Trim the binding ends with a straight cut so the overlap is exactly the same distance as the cut width of your binding strips. (If your binding strips are 2¼" wide, the overlap should be 2¼"; for 2½"-wide binding, the overlap should be 2½".)

2¼" overlap

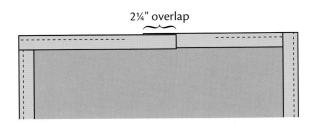

7. Unfold the two ends of the binding and place the tails right sides together so they form a right angle as shown. Draw a diagonal line from corner to corner and pin the strips together.

Draw diagonal line.
Pin ends together.

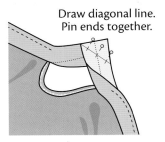

8. Sew along the diagonal line, trim the seam allowance to ¼", and press the seam open. Refold the binding and press. Align the raw edges of the binding with the edge of the quilt top and finish sewing. Start sewing ½" back into the previous stitching and continue sewing ½" past the stitching at the beginning.

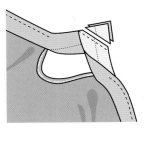

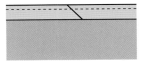

9. Turn the binding to the back of the quilt to cover the machine stitching line. Hand sew the binding in place, mitering the corners when you come to them.

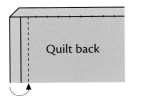

Quilt back

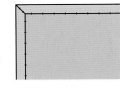

Signing Your Quilt

Make a label that includes your name, the city and state where you lived when you made the quilt, and the date you finished. If someone else did the quilting or some other part of the quilt, give his or her name, city, and state as well. Does this quilt have a name? Was it given to someone as a gift and for what occasion? Was it made for a special purpose? These are all things you can add to your label. When the information is complete, turn the raw edges under and blindstitch the label to the back of your quilt.

"Beautiful Butterfly" Antenna Pattern. Project on page 24.

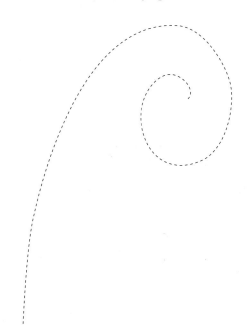

Bibliography

Brackman, Barbara. *Encyclopedia of Pieced Quilt Patterns*. Paducah, KY: American Quilter's Society, 1993.

Encyclopedia of Classic Quilt Patterns. Birmingham, AL: Oxmoor House, Inc., 2001.

Gordon, Maggi McCormick. *1000 Great Quilt Blocks*. Woodinville, WA: Martingale & Company, 2003.

Hopkins, Judy. *Around the Block with Judy Hopkins*. Woodinville, WA: Martingale & Company, 1994.

———. *Around the Block Again: More Rotary-Cut Blocks from Judy Hopkins*. Woodinville, WA: Martingale & Company, 2000.

———. *Once More around the Block*. Woodinville, WA: Martingale & Company, 2003.

Malone, Maggie. *5,500 Quilt Block Designs*. New York: Sterling Publishing Co., Inc., 2004.

Martin, Nancy J. *365 Quilt Blocks a Year*. Woodinville, WA: Martingale & Company, 1999.

McCloskey, Marsha. *Block Party: A Quilter's Extravaganza of 120 Rotary-Cut Block Patterns*. Emmaus, PA: Rodale Inc., 1998.

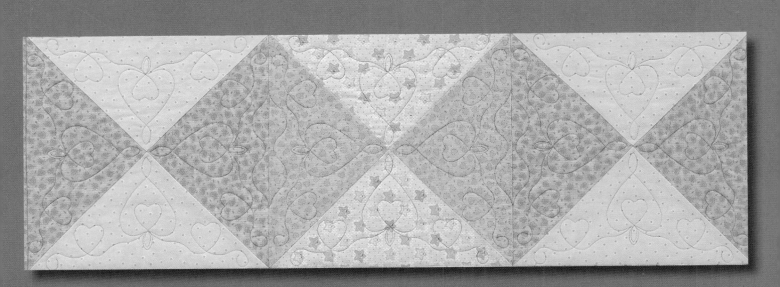

About the Author

LAURIE BEVAN enjoys designing quilts with traditional blocks, and there are so many wonderful blocks to choose from. Different block layouts, sashings, borders, and other design elements turn standard blocks into beautiful new quilt designs. For Laurie, it's all about the fabric. Using large pieces in simple block designs, she lets the fabric do the work for her. Why cut these great fabrics into tiny pieces?

Laurie's first book, *Lickety-Split Quilts: Fast Projects from BIG Blocks*, was also published by Martingale & Company, and she is very proud of its success. She launched her new pattern company, Wonderland Quilts, in 2006 and is excited to watch it grow.

Laurie is also busy running Wonderland Retreats, a quilters' retreat house in Poulsbo, Washington. She enjoys meeting quilters from all over the country and is pleased that they always have a wonderful time.

From the quilting studio in her home on Hood Canal in Washington State, Laurie enjoys designing and sewing, sometimes reading or knitting, but always watching the beautiful changing scenery outside her window. Visit her at www.wonderlandquilts.com or wonderlandretreats.com.

NEW AND BESTSELLING TITLES FROM

America's Best-Loved Craft & Hobby Books®
America's Best-Loved Knitting Books®

America's Best-Loved Quilt Books®

APPLIQUÉ
Adoration Quilts
Appliqué at Play
Appliqué Takes Wing
Favorite Quilts from Anka's Treasures
Garden Party
Mimi Dietrich's Baltimore Basics
Stitch and Split Appliqué
Sunbonnet Sue and Scottie Too—*New!*
Tea in the Garden

FOCUS ON WOOL
Hooked on Wool
Needle Felting—*New!*
Simply Primitive

GENERAL QUILTMAKING
All Buttoned Up
Bound for Glory—*New!*
Calendar Kids
Colorful Quilts—*New!*
Creating Your Perfect Quilting Space
Creative Quilt Collection Volume Two
Dazzling Quilts
A Dozen Roses—*New!*
Follow-the-Line Quilting Designs
Follow-the-Line Quilting Designs
    Volume Two
A Fresh Look at Seasonal Quilts
Modern Primitive Quilts—*New!*
Positively Postcards—*New!*
Posterize It!—*New!*
Prairie Children and Their Quilts
Quilt Revival
Quilter's Block-a-Day Calendar—*New!*
Quilting in the Country—*New!*
Sensational Sashiko
Simple Traditions
Twice Quilted—*New!*

LEARNING TO QUILT
The Blessed Home Quilt
Color for the Terrified Quilter—*New!*
Happy Endings, Revised Edition
Let's Quilt!
The Magic of Quiltmaking
The Quilter's Quick Reference Guide
Your First Quilt Book (or it should be!)

PAPER PIECING
300 Paper-Pieced Quilt Blocks
Easy Machine Paper Piecing
Show Me How to Paper Piece
**Showstopping Quilts to Foundation
    Piece**—*New!*
Spellbinding Quilts

PIECING
40 Fabulous Quick-Cut Quilts
Better by the Dozen
Big 'n Easy
Clever Quarters, Too
Lickety-Split Quilts
New Cuts for New Quilts
Over Easy
Sew One and You're Done
Snowball Quilts
Square Deal—*New!*
Stack a New Deck
Sudoku Quilts
Two-Block Theme Quilts
Twosey-Foursey Quilts
Wheel of Mystery Quilts

QUILTS FOR BABIES & CHILDREN
Even More Quilts for Baby
**The Little Box of Baby Quilts
    —New!**
More Quilts for Baby
Quilts for Baby
Sweet and Simple Baby Quilts

SCRAP QUILTS
More Nickel Quilts
Nickel Quilts
Save the Scraps
Scraps of Time
Simple Strategies for Scrap Quilts
Successful Scrap Quilts from Simple
    Rectangles
A Treasury of Scrap Quilts

CRAFTS
Bag Boutique
Creative Embellishments—*New!*
Greeting Cards Using Digital Photos
It's a Wrap
**The Little Box of Beaded Bracelets
    and Earrings**—*New!*
**The Little Box of Beaded Necklaces
    and Earrings**—*New!*
Miniature Punchneedle Embroidery
A Passion for Punchneedle
Scrapbooking Off the Page…and on the Wall
Sculpted Threads—*New!*

KNITTING & CROCHET
365 Knitting Stitches a Year:
    Perpetual Calendar
A to Z of Knitting—*New!*
Crochet from the Heart
Crocheted Pursenalities—*New!*
First Crochet
First Knits
Fun and Funky Crochet
Funky Chunky Knitted Accessories
Handknit Style II
The Knitter's Book of Finishing
    Techniques
Knitting with Gigi—*New!*
The Little Box of Crochet for Baby—*New!*
The Little Box of Knitted Throws
Modern Classics
More Sensational Knitted Socks—*New!*
Pursenalities
Silk Knits
Top Down Sweaters—*New!*
Wrapped in Comfort—*New!*
The Yarn Stash Workbook

Our books are available at bookstores and your favorite craft, fabric,
and yarn retailers. If you don't see the title you're looking for,
visit us at **www.martingale-pub.com** or contact us at:

1-800-426-3126

International: 1-425-483-3313 • **Fax:** 1-425-486-7596 • **Email:** info@martingale-pub.com

3/07